SPACE

LIGHT

STRUCTURE

SPACE

LIGHT

STRUCTURE

The Jewelry of **Margaret De Patta**

URSULA ILSE-NEUMAN

JULIE M. MUÑIZ

Museum of Arts and Design, New York, New York
Oakland Museum of California, Oakland, California
2012

Museum of Arts and Design
2 Columbus Circle
New York, New York 10019
www.madmuseum.org

museum of arts and design

Oakland Museum of California
1000 Oak Street
Oakland, California 94607
www.museumca.org

Exhibition Schedule
Space, Light, Structure: The Jewelry of Margaret De Patta is the catalogue for the exhibition organized by the Museum of Arts and Design and the Oakland Museum of California. The exhibition is on view at the Oakland Museum from February 4 through May 13, 2012, and at the Museum of Arts and Design from June 12 to September 23, 2012.

Published in the United States of America by the Museum of Arts and Design and the Oakland Museum of California.

Printed in the United States of America by Capital Offset Co., Inc., Concord, New Hampshire, on acid-free paper, and typeset in *Fedra*, designed by Peter Bílak; *National*, designed by Kris Sowersby; and *Galaxy Polaris*, designed by Chester Jenkins.

ISBN: 978-1-890385-21-7

Library of Congress Control Number: 2011943994

Sponsors
Space, Light, Structure: The Jewelry of Margaret De Patta was made possible in part by generous support from the Terra Foundation for American Art, the Rotasa Foundation, and the National Endowment for the Arts. Research for this project was supported by a Craft Research Fund grant from the Center for Craft, Creativity & Design, a Center of the University of North Carolina at Asheville.

EDITOR

Nancy Preu

BOOK DESIGN

HvADesign, NY
Henk van Assen with
Lisa Mangano and
Anna Zhang

FRONT COVER

Barbara Cannon Myers (b. 1929)
Portrait of Margaret De Patta, c. 1955
4 ¼ x 5 ⅛ in. (10.8 x 13 cm)
Margaret De Patta Archives, Bielawski Trust, Point Richmond, California

BACK COVER (TOP)

Margaret De Patta
Jewelry as photographed by the artist, c. 1941
Margaret De Patta Archives, Bielawski Trust, Point Richmond, California

BACK COVER (LOWER LEFT)

Margaret De Patta
Pin, c. 1947–50
sterling silver, coral, malachite
2 ¾ x 3 ⅜ x ⅜ in. (69.9 x 85.7 x 9.5 mm)
Museum of Arts and Design, New York, Gift of Eugene Bielawski, The Margaret De Patta Bequest, through the American Craft Council, 1976

BACK COVER (LOWER RIGHT)

Margaret De Patta
Pin, 1956
sterling silver, quartz, epoxy enamel paint
1 ⅞ x 3 ¾ x ½ in. (47.6 x 95.3 x 12.7 mm)
Collection of the Oakland Museum of California, Gift of Eugene Bielawski, The Margaret De Patta Memorial Collection

ENDPAPERS

Margaret De Patta
De Patta Originals, c. 1949
black-and-white photograph
7 ¼ x 8 ¼ in. (18.4 x 21 cm)
Margaret De Patta Archives, Bielawski Trust, Point Richmond, California

All measurements: height x width x depth, unless otherwise noted.

Contents

07 **Foreword**
HOLLY HOTCHNER

09 **Foreword**
LORI FOGARTY

11 ACKNOWLEDGMENTS

12 LENDERS, SPONSORS, AND DONORS

16 **Margaret De Patta** A Modernist's Vision
URSULA ILSE-NEUMAN

56 **Balancing Act** Margaret De Patta
and Constructivism
GLENN ADAMSON

76 Plates

108 **Jewelry for a Never-Increasing Minority**
Margaret De Patta in the Marketplace
JULIE M. MUÑIZ

130 TIMELINE AND SELECTED EXHIBITION HISTORY

140 BIBLIOGRAPHY

142 INDEX

144 PHOTO CREDITS

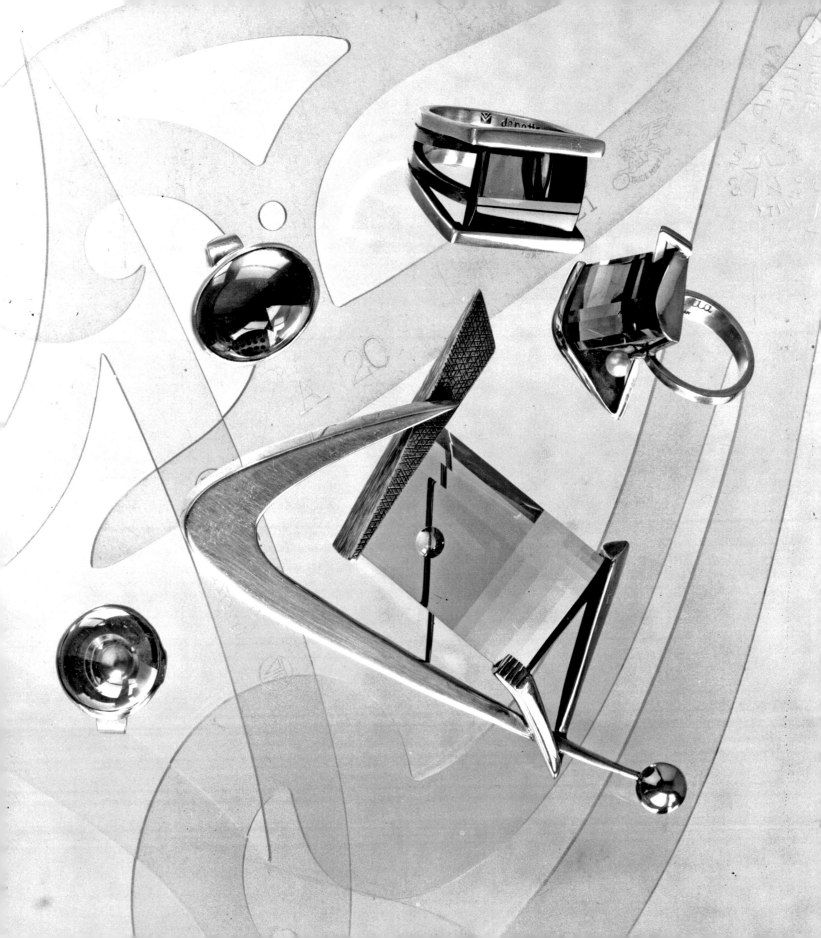

Foreword

Margaret De Patta was every bit an artist of her time. Her cerebral jewelry expresses her own evolving aesthetic and social philosophy as it unfolded over four decades of enormous change in American society—from the Roaring Twenties through the Great Depression, World War II, and the prosperity and menacing Cold War fears of the 1950s and 1960s. Nearly half a century after her death, *Space, Light, Structure: The Jewelry of Margaret De Patta* focuses for the first time on her complete oeuvre, providing insight into the importance of her association with Hungarian-born Constructivist László Moholy-Nagy and the Chicago Bauhaus ideals that influenced her approach as a maker and thinker.

The collaboration of the Museum of Arts and Design and the Oakland Museum of California on this tribute to Margaret De Patta is uniquely appropriate. Each of our institutions played a part in the artist's career, each remains dedicated to celebrating her achievements, and each treasures important De Patta jewelry in its collection.

Many individuals and organizations deserve recognition for their invaluable assistance in making this exhibition and its accompanying publication possible. We are grateful to MAD curator of jewelry Ursula Ilse-Neuman for her singular vision in initiating this project and seeing it through its many challenges. Her tenure at the museum has been hallmarked by the many groundbreaking exhibitions she has organized and the numerous publications in which she has revealed her remarkable insights into contemporary art. In the lead essay for *Space, Light, Structure,* Ilse-Neuman adroitly examines the artistic, personal, and societal forces that converged to make De Patta's life and work memorable. Craft historian and theorist Glenn Adamson focuses in on the ideas and visions of Constructivism as espoused at the Chicago Bauhaus, particularly by László Moholy-Nagy, and skillfully relates them to De Patta's work. Finally, OMCA curator Julie M. Muñiz details the triumphs and failures in De Patta's ambitious attempt to turn her democratic beliefs in affordable, serially produced jewelry into a working reality.

Space, Light, Structure: The Jewelry of Margaret De Patta embodies the Museum of Arts and Design's mission to explore the rich intersection of art, craft, and design in the twentieth and twenty-first centuries

and to herald underrecognized artists. Such major undertakings cannot be accomplished without the guidance and encouragement of David McFadden, the Museum's chief curator, who was an early and stalwart supporter of the project. Thanks are also owed to Dorothy Globus, Exhibitions Curator; Judi Kamien, Director of Institutional Giving; Brian MacFarland, Vice President of Education; Brian Mac-Elhose, Associate Registrar; and the entire Museum staff, as well as the interns and volunteers on whose work we depend day in and day out. Among the many MAD staff members who have helped to make the exhibition and publication a success, it is essential to single out curatorial assistant Jane Ro, whose dedication was instrumental in managing the many details of the project from its inception. Finally, our deep appreciation goes to Nancy Preu, discerning editor of many of MAD's publications, as well as to Henk van Assen, the creative eye behind this beautiful publication, and Rupert Deese, whose installation eloquently responds to De Patta's fascination with space, light, and structure, bringing her timeless vision to a twenty-first century audience.

When sponsorship of a project comes with personal involvement, that funding means twice as much. I would like to thank the Terra Foundation for American Art, and in particular Carrie Haslett, for its early commitment to and extremely generous support of the exhibition's organization and presentation at MAD. I would also like to thank the National Endowment for the Arts, the Rotasa Foundation, and the Center for Craft, Creativity & Design at the University of North Carolina Asheville for their thoughtful and significant commitment to the project. My gratitude extends, as well, to Kim and Al Eiber, David Charak, Susan Grant Lewin, and several other long-time friends of MAD for their support of this book.

Lastly, it is imperative to thank our Board of Trustees—led by Chairman Lewis Kruger, vital and steadfast benefactor Nanette Laitman, Chairman Emeritus Jerome A. Chazen, and Chairman Emerita Barbara Tober—for its unwavering support and belief in the Museum and its mission.

HOLLY HOTCHNER, NANETTE L. LAITMAN DIRECTOR
Museum of Arts and Design, New York

Foreword

The Oakland Museum of California is honored and pleased to partner with the Museum of Arts and Design on this important catalogue and exhibition of the work of jewelry artist Margaret De Patta. OMCA's collection of De Patta jewelry is the largest in the world, having more than seventy-five outstanding pieces that span more than three decades of the artist's career. In addition, OMCA houses De Patta's sketchbooks, accounting records, and other ephemera, valuable archival material for the study of studio jewelry. Most of the De Patta jewelry in the museum's collection was generously donated in 1967 by Eugene Bielawski, De Patta's husband, in memory of his late wife. Important pieces were also given by the artist's friends, who were eager to honor her contributions to the development of studio craft. In gratitude for these gifts, OMCA presented a small exhibition of Margaret De Patta's work in 1976, and examples of her jewelry are continually featured in the museum's Gallery of California Art.

When De Patta turned her attention from painting to jewelry making, there were few precedents in the United States for creating jewelry that expressed the principles of high modernism and the democratic values of the Bauhaus movement. De Patta faced difficult challenges in realizing her dreams, and her work demanded profound dedication. Through *Space, Light, Structure: The Jewelry of Margaret De Patta*, we honor her deeply held commitment to her work and applaud the sheer beauty and boldness of her wearable sculptures.

On behalf of the Oakland Museum of California, I wish to express sincere thanks to Ursula Ilse-Neuman of MAD and Julie M. Muñiz of OMCA for the remarkable exhibition they have organized, as well as for the informative essays they have contributed to this catalogue. Our appreciation also extends to Glenn Adamson for his essay placing De Patta's work within the Constructivist movement.

The exhibition and catalogue for *Space, Light, Structure: The Jewelry of Margaret De Patta* would not have been possible without the generosity of the Terra and Rotasa Foundations, the National Endowment for the Arts, and the Center for Craft, Creativity & Design. Among our local supporters, the Oakland Museum Women's Board must be acknowledged for its role in making the museum's partnership with MAD possible. In addition, OMCA's entire staff must be thanked for their hard work on this project. Finally, we offer our gratitude to our partners at MAD. We are pleased to have Margaret De Patta's jewelry appreciated nationally and internationally.

LORI FOGARTY, EXECUTIVE DIRECTOR
Oakland Museum of California

ACKNOWLEDGMENTS

Space, Light, Structure: The Jewelry of Margaret De Patta became a reality through the help and support of many dedicated colleagues and collaborators.

We would like to thank our colleagues at MAD and OMCA for all of their hard work and support, without which we would have been unable to bring this exhibition to life. Our deep appreciation goes to Holly Hotchner, Nanette L. Laitman Director at MAD; Lori Fogarty, Executive Director at OMCA; and David McFadden, William and Mildred Lasdon Chief Curator and Vice President for Collections and Exhibitions, for their steadfast encouragement. Maggie Pico, OMCA Director of Resource and Enterprise; Ariel Weintraub, OMCA Institutional Giving Manager; Judith Kamien, MAD Director of Institutional Giving; and Katie Gerlach, MAD Associate Development Officer, were untiring in raising support for the exhibition, and we are grateful for their success.

A very special thanks goes to curatorial assistant Jane Ro, who managed the myriad details of the exhibition and catalogue at the Museum of Arts and Design with great diligence and enthusiasm while ably collaborating with staff and interns at the Oakland Museum of California. Her professional know-how greatly contributed to the success of the project.

Dorothy Globus, Curator of Exhibitions, ably oversaw the MAD installation. OMCA registrars Joy Tahan and Valerie Huaco and MAD associate registrars Brian MacElhose and Alisha Ferrin assured safe packing and transport. Nurit Einik, MAD Assistant Curator, played an important role in coordinating the exhibition tour. OMCA staff members Kathy Borgogno, Debra Peterson, and Rachael Zink provided continuous administrative and registration support. The education departments led by Brian MacFarland at MAD and Barbara Henry at OMCA created a range of memorable public programs.

Martha Bielawski's support of the project was invaluable. Her hospitality during numerous visits in which she gave us free access to the precious De Patta archival material is deeply appreciated.

We are grateful to Hattula Moholy-Nagy for supporting the project from the very beginning. Our thanks also go to collectors and lenders to the exhibition Leland Rice and Susan Ehrens for sharing their research and knowledge; Edgar Bartolucci, former Chicago Bauhaus student, for his insightful discussion about the activities at this institution; Patricia Riveron Lee for generously providing a photograph of Francisco Rebajes's wall reliefs; and Steven Cabella for sharing his immense knowledge of the period. In addition, a special thank you goes to several colleagues and friends of Margaret De Patta who openly discussed their memories of her, including Merry Renk, Florence Resnikoff, Avis Blanchette, Dick Sperisen, Peter Levy, Karin Solomon, and Tanya Lazar.

We offer warm thanks to the Center for Craft, Creativity & Design for funding two Windgate Fellows at OMCA. Jennifer Shaifer (OMCA Windgate Fellow, 2009) and Alicia Arroyo (OMCA Windgate Fellow, 2010) conducted crucial research and provided unstinting assistance on the project.

We are deeply appreciative, as well, of Mija Riedel, who undertook initial research at the De Patta Archives, and of MAD curatorial assistant Maya Jimenez. In particular, we thank Pamela McCleave for her diligent work securing and organizing image rights; Allison Condo, Cooper-Hewitt–Parsons master's program intern, for her dedicated research; and Jennifer Hinshaw, who carried out research on mid-century craft galleries. In addition, Grace Lee, Michelle Woo, Emily Levine, Elizabeth Maxwell, Jennifer Hafez, Kathy Fredenburg, Julia Avery-Shapiro, Wendi Parson, Ruth Bruno, and Shelley Selim must be thanked for their enthusiasm and hard work.

Finally, our heartfelt appreciation goes to the institutions, foundations, galleries, and public and private donors who supported this exhibition and publication and whose names are listed on the following page.

Ursula Ilse-Neuman | Museum of Arts and Design
Julie M. Muñiz | Oakland Museum of California

LENDERS, SPONSORS, AND DONORS

INSTITUTIONAL LENDERS

Akron Art Museum, Akron, Ohio

Archives of American Art, Smithsonian Institution, Washington, D.C.

Art Institute of Chicago, Chicago, Illinois

Bauhaus-Archiv, Berlin, Germany

Dallas Museum of Art, Dallas, Texas

Metal Arts Guild of the Bay Area, San Francisco, California

Montreal Museum of Fine Arts, Montreal, Quebec

Museum of Fine Arts, Boston, Boston, Massachusetts

Museum of Modern Art, New York, New York

Renwick Gallery of the Smithsonian American Art Museum, Washington, D.C.

Smithsonian American Art Museum, Washington, D.C.

Solomon R. Guggenheim Museum, New York, New York

Tacoma Art Museum, Tacoma, Washington

University of Michigan Art Museum, Ann Arbor, Michigan

PRIVATE LENDERS

Ruth Asawa

Merrill C. Berman

Martha Bielawski

Toby Bielawski

Avis Blanchette estate

Steven Cabella

Kenneth Dukoff

Frances Archipenko Gray

Allen Hunter

Forrest L. Merrill

Hattula Moholy-Nagy

Leland Rice and **Susan Ehrens**

Leslie Simons

Karin L. Solomon estate

Janet Zapata

GALLERY LENDERS

Andrea Rosen Gallery, New York, New York

Bruce Silverstein Gallery, New York, New York

Ubu Gallery, New York & **Barry Friedman Limited,** New York

INSTITUTIONAL SPONSORS

Center for Craft, Creativity & Design, a Center of the University of North Carolina at Asheville, Hendersonville, North Carolina

Collectors Circle, Museum of Arts and Design, New York, New York

National Endowment for the Arts, Washington, D.C.

Oakland Museum of California Art Guild, Oakland, California

Oakland Museum of California Women's Board, Oakland, California

Rotasa Foundation, Mill Valley, California

Terra Foundation for American Art, Chicago, Illinois

PRIVATE DONORS

David Charak II

Kim and Al Eiber

Susan Grant Lewin

Florence Resnikoff

Phyllis Weber-Levine

"It was my good to come along the opportune

+ crystal -

fortune
historically at
time..."

Margaret De Patta

A Modernist's Vision

URSULA ILSE-NEUMAN

Introduction

Margaret De Patta (1903–1964) was a young girl attending high school in San Diego during the years after World War I when László Moholy-Nagy (1895–1946) and a group of highly sophisticated men and women were revolutionizing art and design a world away at the Bauhaus school in Weimar, Germany. Just two decades later, dramatic world events would bring these two visionaries together in the United States, and the concept of light and motion they shared would be realized in Margaret De Patta's transcendent new jewelry form.

Trained as a painter in the 1920s when avant-garde European art movements were beginning to influence California artists, De Patta's interest in three-dimensional composition and architecture moved her away from the flat canvas to a sculptural form she could make her own. She envisioned a piece of jewelry as a

dynamic object that could influence perception of space and movement by creating reflections, optical illusions, and unexpected alterations of light. "The fascination of looking into or through an object or material is boundless," De Patta declared. "Add the excitement of optical effects such as magnification, reduction, multiplication, distortion and image reflection, and the function of the gemstone in jewelry becomes one to stimulate the ingenuity and imagination of the designer." [1]

De Patta's bold, yet meticulously conceived, brooches, pendants, and rings signaled a radical departure from the prevailing concept of jewelry as mere body ornament. Determined to create an art reflective of her time, she rejected moribund traditional jewelry designs and practices and, with technical mastery, aligned her jewelry with modernist design aesthetics as she aligned her life with the philosophy and social agenda of the German Bauhaus as reborn in the United States.

Stimulated by the cultural, social, and technological changes that were transforming life in the San Francisco Bay Area and American society as a whole during the decades around World War II, De Patta played a pivotal role in promoting the concept of jewelry as sophisticated wearable art. As a teacher and formative member of an expanding community of California artists and craftsmen, she became a seminal figure in the emergence and growth of American studio jewelry. Through her dedicated efforts to fulfill the Bauhaus ideal of making well-designed low-cost jewelry that would reach a new and larger audience, and her unsurpassed one-of-a-kind creations, her legacy includes crucial contributions to the field and a body of work that remains fresh and vital today.

FIGURE 1
Barbara Cannon Myers (b. 1929)
Portrait of Margaret De Patta, c. 1955
4¼ x 5⅛ in. (10.8 x 13 cm)
Margaret De Patta Archives, Bielawski Trust,
Point Richmond, California

Artistic Beginning, 1903–1929

Born in 1903 in Tacoma, Washington, Margaret De Patta (née Mary Margaret Strong) was seven years old when her family moved to San Diego, California. Evidencing an early interest in art, after graduating from high school in 1921, she studied painting and sculpture at the Academy of Fine Arts in San Diego for two years and continued her training at the California School of Fine Arts in San Francisco from 1923 to 1925. During her student years she developed an affinity for contemporary art through exposure to the strong modernist presence in California.[2] The first major exhibition of modern art in California was presented at the 1915 Panama-Pacific International Exposition. In the 1920s the adventurous Oakland Art Gallery, the California Palace of the Legion of Honor, and the Mills College Art Gallery all brought exhibitions of artwork by European modernists to the Bay Area.[3] A strong women's movement had developed in California, with women winning the right to vote on a state level in 1911. The presence of a community of women actively interested in avant-garde art and ideas significantly influenced De Patta's development as an artist.

De Patta won a scholarship to the prestigious Art Students League in New York City, where she studied painting in 1929 with urban realist painter and influential teacher Kenneth Hayes Miller (1876–1952), who encouraged her to visit galleries displaying art by leading European modernists.[4] A painting with shaded three-dimensional shapes that convey a sense of volume and depth on the flat picture plane reveals her early interest in abstract spatial design (fig. 2).

The trajectory of De Patta's career in modernist jewelry began to emerge when she returned to California in 1929 and sought a

FIGURE 2
Margaret De Patta
Untitled, c. 1917–21
gouache on paper
13 ½ x 10 in. (34.3 x 25.4 cm)
Margaret De Patta Archives, Bielawski Trust,
Point Richmond, California

wedding ring for her marriage to San Francisco department store executive Samuel De Patta.[5] Her frustration in locating a wedding band that reflected her preference for contemporary design is often recounted as the event that changed her life and the course of American studio jewelry.[6] She went to the Art Copper Shop in San Francisco and asked Armin Hairenian (1892–1981), a well-known Armenian metalsmith and jeweler, to make a wedding band for her, but his ring was far from the modernist design she sought. Demonstrating an early resolve, she asked him to teach her how to make the ring she envisioned. Although Hairenian did instruct De Patta on technique, he had little interest in helping her explore unconventional design ideas, and her "apprenticeship" lasted just two months.[7]

At a time when jewelry was either a costly luxury item, an unrefined craft object, or a piece of mass-produced jewelry with conventional forms and settings, De Patta was determined to apply her creative energy to making a new kind of contemporary jewelry, despite the fact that few jewelers or metalworkers shared her interest.[8] Undaunted by the absence of formal training programs, she turned to books on jewelry making, noting, "This is an old craft. . . . Hundreds of books have been written on it, and I've read every one of them from the public library—many of them several times."[9]

A De Patta Style Emerges, 1929—1939

While continuing to paint, De Patta turned to museum collections of Egyptian, Turkish, Etruscan, and Mayan jewelry for inspiration. The influence of ethnic pieces is apparent in her 1930 pendant in sterling silver with Persian turquoise (fig.3). She incorporated new skills as she acquired them, applying her

study of engraving at a watch-making school in 1932, for example, to a bracelet she made around 1933 (fig. 5).[10] Finally, in 1934, De Patta ceased painting altogether and set up a workshop in her kitchen so she could focus on producing jewelry.

Most likely, it was the opportunity to work out concepts of space in three dimensions that encouraged De Patta to move from painting to jewelry making, for she quickly left ethnic and historical jewelry influences behind and became one of the earliest American jewelers to take inspiration from modern art. The resemblance to African masks evident in a ring she made around 1934 (fig. 4) suggests her interest in the Cubist visual vocabulary, in which Primitivism played an early part. In 1952, looking back on the changes that she helped to bring about, De Patta observed, "The field of jewelry has gone through the same repudiation of old forms, re-examination of function and exploration of its physical materials as have all other creative fields since the rebellion of the Futurists and Cubists. The throwing overboard of traditional forms has opened up the entire world of creative exploration in materials, technics [sic], and contemporary concepts."[11]

In order to realize her designs with an economy of means, she began working with basic metal sheets, creating an endless assortment of shapes by beating, cutting, and sawing metal pieces. She used a torch to melt the ends of wire and bits of metal into beads and then assembled these components into wearable pieces, occasionally adding interest with drilled or pierced holes. Her sterling silver pin from around 1934 was constructed from such an assortment of diverse components (fig. 7). De Patta arrived at this dynamic and visually arresting composition by contrasting light and shadow and offsetting straight lines against curves.

FIGURE 3
Margaret De Patta
Pendant, 1930
sterling silver, Persian turquoise
3¼ x 1⅞ x ⅜ in. (83 x 48 x 10 mm), without chain
Collection of the Oakland Museum of California,
Gift of Eugene Bielawski, The Margaret De Patta Memorial Collection

FIGURE 4
Margaret De Patta
Ring, c. 1934
sterling silver
1⅝ x ⅞ x ⅞ in.
(41 x 22 x 22 mm)
Collection of Janet Zapata

FIGURE 5
Margaret De Patta
Bracelet, c. 1933
sterling silver, turquoise
1½ x 2½ x 1¼ in. (38 x 64 x 32 mm)
Collection of the Oakland
Museum of California,
Gift of Eugene Bielawski,
The Margaret De Patta Memorial
Collection

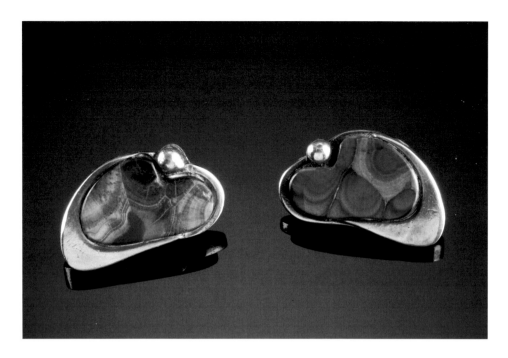

FIGURE 6
Margaret De Patta
Earrings, 1941
sterling silver, malachite
½ x ⅞ x ½ in. (13 x 22 x 13 mm)
Collection of the Oakland Museum of California,
Gift of Mrs. Lange Steeves

Convinced that modern design should be aligned with modern architecture, her jewelry increasingly became investigations of formal relationships emphasizing open structures and transparency. As she later stated, "Problems common to sculpture and architecture are inherent in jewelry design, i.e., space, form, tension, organic structure, scale, texture interpenetration, superimposition, and economy of means, each necessary element playing its role in a unified entity."[12]

By 1935, De Patta was recognized as an accomplished professional jeweler with a growing following, even at the height of the Great Depression. Her work frequently appeared in major exhibitions in the Bay Area, the most notable of which was the 1939 Golden Gate International Exposition in San Francisco, an event that promoted modernism and afforded women prominent roles as organizers and exhibitors.[13] De Patta's distinctive aesthetic emphasized the integrity of the overall composition in contrast to traditional jewelry designs that often sacrificed balance through the use of unstylish or clumsy mountings designed to show off gemstones. Perhaps initially motivated by the restrictive costs of precious materials, De Patta was determined to counter the idea that the value of jewelry was based on the inclusion of costly gems and metals; instead, she used modest materials, masterfully incorporating them into artistic compositions.

Over the course of her career, De Patta's ingenuity in integrating mountings, fastenings, and clasps into her compositions became a distinctive characteristic of virtually all of her jewelry. Her skill is already apparent in earrings from 1941, where she cleverly attached malachite to the post through a silver ball that functions both structurally and visually (fig. 6). De Patta considered earrings to be the most personal of all jewelry forms, and these earrings display her sensitivity to the wearer. Successful in both form and function, they reflect her attraction to the abstract, organic forms of biomorphism that were an important influence on the art and design of the time,[14] and they conform

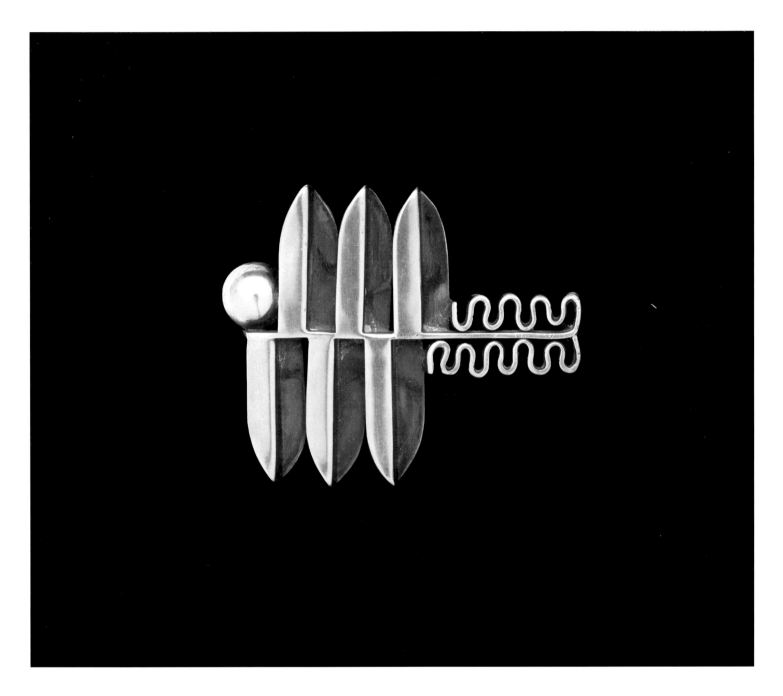

FIGURE 7
Margaret De Patta
Pin, c. 1934
sterling silver
2 x 2⅞ x ¼ in. (51 x 73 x 6 mm)
The Dukoff Collection

FIGURE 8 [LEFT]
Margaret De Patta
Pin, 1937
sterling silver
2½ x 1¼ x ⅞ in. (64 x 32 x 22 mm)
The Dukoff Collection

FIGURE 9 [BELOW]
Margaret De Patta
Ring, 1940
sterling silver
1¼ x 1 x ¾ in. (32 x 25 x 19 mm)
The Dukoff Collection

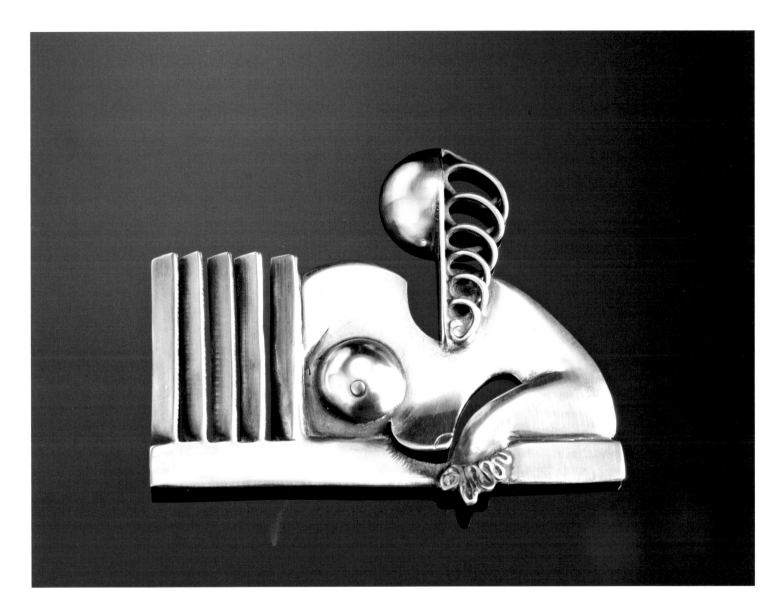

FIGURE 10
Margaret De Patta
Saskia at the Window, 1933
sterling silver
2 x 2¾ in. (51 x 70 mm)
Collection of the Oakland Museum of California,
Gift of Eugene Bielawski, The Margaret De Patta
Memorial Collection

to the shape of the ear. De Patta often drew on biomorphism's more natural shapes to soften the hard-edged, architectural shapes in her Constructivist compositions.

A typical example of De Patta's work in this period is the deceptively simple silver pin from around 1937, a demonstration of her growing ability to assemble basic shapes and create a sense of depth and visual interest within a carefully conceived, unified whole (fig. 8). The intriguing 1933 piece *Saskia at the Window* (fig. 10), originally made to adorn a hand mirror, is unusual for its abstracted reference to the human figure, which De Patta explored for a brief period at this early stage.

A Turning Point: Moholy-Nagy, 1939—1940

De Patta was restless to broaden her exposure to art and architecture through lectures and travel. In 1936, Margaret and Sam De Patta traveled to Mexico (fig. 11), where she filled a journal with notes, sketches, and photographs that chronicled her admiration for that country's modern architecture. Touring the Bauhaus-inspired Centro Escolar Revolución, with its curved corners and prominent horizontal bands (fig. 12), she labeled it "the finest modern building I have seen."

It is very likely that De Patta attended or read the transcript of the well-publicized lecture on Bauhaus education that Hungarian-born artist and designer László Moholy-Nagy presented at the annual convention of the Pacific Arts Association in San Francisco in April 1939.[15] Moholy-Nagy had been the principal proponent of the Constructivist[16] movement in Germany and a Bauhaus master when, as a Jew and "decadent" artist, he was forced to leave the country in 1928 because of Nazi suppression. He was working in London in 1936 when the Association of Arts and Industries in Chicago invited him to come to the United States and open a new school based on Bauhaus principles. Moholy-Nagy later commented, "It was clear to all of us who knew the organic structure of the Bauhaus idea that after the curtailment of freedom in Europe only America offered the atmosphere in which to continue the task."[17]

The New Bauhaus opened its doors on October 18, 1937, and its first mission statement hailed Constructivism as "the art of our century, its mirror and its voice, in which form and substance are one."[18] When the original school closed due to financial difficulties, Moholy-Nagy opened the School of Design in February 1939 and traveled the country promoting the Bauhaus goal of training artists, designers, and craftspeople to create superior industrial design that was also affordable.

In his lecture, Moholy-Nagy chronicled the revolutionary impact of the Bauhaus and spoke of a new design aesthetic emphasizing transparency. He described the School of Design's preliminary course as the first phase in a new art education that integrated craftsmanship, technology, and science, but emphasized that "art itself cannot be taught, only the way to do it."[19] For the first time in the history of Chicago, a course was devoted to light as a material of creative construction.[20] In addition to courses in drawing, photography, and the basic sciences, the school offered lectures in art history, philosophy, and psychology so that students would develop into well-rounded individuals suited for modern society.

FIGURE 11
Margaret De Patta
Page from Margaret De Patta's Mexico travel journal showing
Margaret and Sam De Patta in Mexico, 1936
6¾ x 4¼ x ¾ in. (17.1 x 10.8 x 1.9 cm)
Margaret De Patta Archives, Bielawski Trust, Point Richmond, California

FIGURE 12
Margaret De Patta
Page from Margaret De Patta's Mexico travel journal showing
Centro Escolar Revolución in Mexico City, 1936
6¾ x 4¼ x ¾ in. (17.1 x 10.8 x 1.9 cm)
Margaret De Patta Archives, Bielawski Trust, Point Richmond, California

In light of her own explorations with coaxing spatial compositions from metal sheets, De Patta must have been riveted by Moholy-Nagy's descriptions of exercises in which students cut and folded flat sheets of paper to create three-dimensional volume: "Everything which has three dimensions has something to do with volume and everything which has something to do with volume has something to do with space. And we believe that we must teach first the fundamentals—material, volume, space— before we can teach practical design for the daily routine."[21] It was as if De Patta had realized the goals of the preliminary course on her own.

It may well have been this lecture that introduced De Patta to camera-less photograms, a new aspect of photography that Moholy-Nagy had begun experimenting with in 1922. Calling himself a light modulator rather than a photographer, he described a simple process of placing objects with different properties on photosensitive paper so that they created shadows and images in varying tones of white and black. To illustrate the unexpected and often spectacular results made by Bauhaus students, he showed slides of photograms they had made in just a few months of experimentation.

De Patta's early use of the photogram to investigate the way light passes through different materials to create abstract spatial relationships can be seen in *Positive Form #15, Squiggles with Black* (fig. 13). An untitled photogram from 1939 (fig. 14) and a pin from around 1955 (fig. 15) show De Patta exploring similar ideas in both two-dimensional and three-dimensional forms. In the pin, she uses a juxtaposition of positive and negative space to create the illusion of interpenetrating planes.

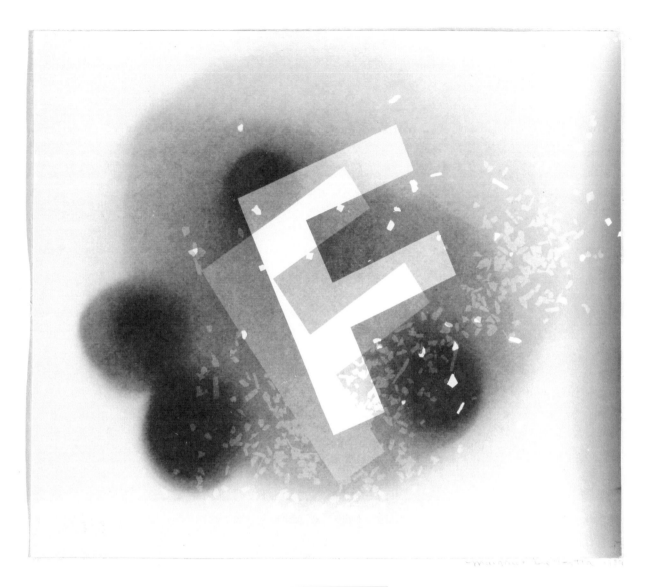

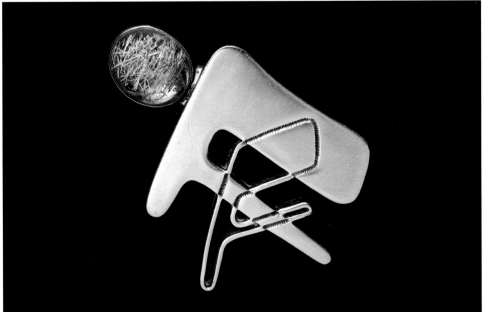

FIGURE 16
Ilya Bolotowsky (1907–1981)
Study for the Hall of Medical Sciences mural at the 1939 World's Fair in New York, 1938–39
oil on canvas
30 x 48 in. (76.2 x 121.9 cm)
The Art Institute of Chicago, American Art, Wilson L. Mead Fund
Art © Estate of Ilya Bolotowsky, licensed by VAGA, New York, NY

FIGURE 17
Francisco Rebajes (1905–1990)
Metal wall reliefs in the Dominican Republic's pavilion at the New York World's Fair, 1939
Collection of Patricia Riveron Lee

Moholy-Nagy went on to explain that in addition to considering solid volume, a designer must consider virtual volume, which originates through motion. "It is clear that besides the static forms the designer has to organize movements in household gadgets, motor cars, and any kinetic devices. We have to think often in terms of motion in our design to be in agreement with the given tasks of our age."[22] De Patta recognized this new avenue in design and was determined to explore it to the fullest. She would later write, "Movement in itself is visually exciting but when it is used to articulate space and to produce definite positive and negative volume relationships it takes on a new vitality and meaning."[23]

Another impressive aspect of Moholy-Nagy's presentation was the revelation that the German Bauhaus was an economic success through the royalties it received from industrial prototypes designed by the metal workshop. In fact, students paid no tuition and received wages from the Bauhaus for the work they produced. Perhaps these facts contributed to De Patta's belief that she would be able to make a financial success with her own designs while adhering to the Bauhaus design principles and social philosophy she came to admire.

In 1939 Margaret and Sam De Patta traveled to the World's Fair in New York City, where, among other wonders of the day, they saw a sizable mural with abstract biomorphic imagery (fig. 16) by the early twentieth-century Russian émigré Ilya Bolotowsky (1907–1981) and large metal reliefs (fig. 17) by Dominican-born sculptor and jewelry artist Francisco Rebajes (1905–1990). On the way to New York, De Patta stopped in Chicago, and her travel journal shows photos of the School of Design with her written note "talked with Moholy-Nagy and decided to take summer course" (fig. 18).[24]

The Bauhaus Influence, Early 1940s

When De Patta returned to San Francisco she attended what has been described as the most significant event in California for art, design, and architecture: the 1940 traveling exhibition *The Bauhaus: How it Worked.* Organized by the Museum of Modern Art in New York, it opened in the Mills College Art Gallery in Oakland and introduced West Coast artists and teachers to modernism and Bauhaus principles. [25]

That summer, Chicago's School of Design faculty came to teach at Mills College, and De Patta enrolled in classes. Led by Moholy-Nagy, the teachers included photographer, theorist and painter György Kepes; painter Robert Jay Wolff; weaver Marli Ehrman; furniture designer Charles Niedringhaus; and artist, designer, and craftsman James Prestini. This high-powered faculty taught courses in drawing, painting, photography, weaving, paper cutting, metalwork, modeling, and casting, all based on the Bauhaus belief in combining intuition and discipline in work that is meaningful in a technological world. A large exhibition at Mills College featured paintings by Moholy-Nagy, photographs by Kepes, trays and bowls by Prestini, and a large wall hanging by Ehrman.

At Mills College, Moholy-Nagy recognized that De Patta's work with transparent stones altered visual perception and exemplified his own concept of "vision in motion." He told her that she was already putting many Bauhaus theories and Constructivist ideas into practice in designs that reflected the logical working out of a structural and spatial problem without extraneous elements.[26] This is evident in her 1941 pin, where she created a unified composition out of sterling silver, moss agate, and black onyx, diverse materials varying in tactility, shape, texture, and

talked with L. Moholy-Nagy and decided to take summer cours[e]

School of Design
247 East Ontario Street, Chicago, Illinois

FIGURE 18
Margaret De Patta
Page from Margaret De Patta's scrapbook showing the School of Design in Chicago, 1940
mixed media
11 x 9 ½ in. (27.9 x 24.1 cm)
Margaret De Patta Archives, Bielawski Trust, Point Richmond, California

FIGURE 19 [UPPER RIGHT]
László Moholy-Nagy critiquing a student's work at the School of Design in Chicago, c. 1941
3¼ x 4 in. (8.1 x 10.5 cm)
Bauhaus-Archiv, Berlin

FIGURE 20 [LOWER RIGHT]
Catalogue for the School of Design in Chicago, c. 1940–41
11½ x 8½ in. (29.2 x 21.6 cm)
Margaret De Patta Archives, Bielawski Trust, Point Richmond, California

transparency (pl. 26). The dynamic shapes and textures of this piece generate the feeling of motion, as though they slipped into this relationship for a moment as they were moving past each other.

De Patta attended the School of Design in Chicago for the 1940–41 academic year (fig.20), a time later described as "the most important episode in her constant qualitative growth as a designer-craftsperson-artist."[27] In sculpture workshops, she gained greater knowledge of materials and the effects of light and movement on color and volume, as well as the effects of shadows cast by metal disks and wire-mesh screens. She repeated the exercise Moholy-Nagy had described in his 1939 San Francisco lecture by creating sculpture with nothing but sheets of paper and scissors (see p.56, fig. 1), and in the Textile Weaving Workshop she extended her experiments with transparency to a multitude of materials, even weaving cellophane and rayon into curtain fabric. Moholy-Nagy's most direct contribution to De Patta's jewelry, however, was probably in the use of gemstones as conveyers of light and motion.

After one year in Chicago, De Patta returned to California just months before the attack on Pearl Harbor in December 1941. During the war years, De Patta's career as a jeweler thrived as aircraft and shipbuilding facilities fueled a booming wartime California economy. When the war ended, several million people moved to the West Coast, and California's artistic community grew as artists, writers, musicians, and composers from all over the country took up residence in the state. This influx of talent quickly changed the focus of California artists from local and regional artistic interests to national and international. Postwar

California modernism was characterized by "a mass conversion to abstraction" [28] in art and design that coincided with the postwar need for efficient, inexpensive, and modern housing.

De Patta now found herself in tune with developments she had anticipated in her own life and career. Incorporating contemporary design influences into her San Francisco home, she converted a hilltop bungalow into a modernist, Bauhaus-inspired residence (figs. 21,22). She designed all of the furniture, draperies, and fabrics for the new interior spaces herself and then had everything made to order (fig. 23).

De Patta's year in Chicago had transformed her artistically and personally. In 1941 she divorced Sam De Patta, and in December 1946 she married industrial designer Eugene Bielawski (1911–2002). Bielawski had been the basic workshop instructor during her time at the School of Design, and when he moved to San Francisco in June 1945 to teach in the art department at the California Labor School, their relationship deepened.

The couple embraced the Bauhaus design philosophy and its democratic social agenda, and together they sought to manifest their beliefs through architecture and interior design projects, teaching, production work, and activities that helped support their artistic community. There was more than a hint of communist thinking in their outlook, and this soon led to controversy in their professional and private lives. The core of their collaboration was De Patta's pioneering work in jewelry, but the inherent conflict between the creation of handcrafted jewelry and their desire to produce jewelry for a broader audience would become increasingly apparent in the years ahead.

Seeing Through Jewelry: Opticuts and Floating Stones

De Patta had introduced light and transparency into her jewelry even before her interaction with the Chicago Bauhaus. In 1939, she began working with San Francisco lapidary Francis Sperisen (1900–1986), who was known for his imaginative gem cuts and his skill in creating unorthodox new shapes to exploit color variations and density.[29] Sperisen created jewelry out of unusual materials not generally employed in lapidary work, such as native California gold ore, spinel, and quartz with mineral inclusions. De Patta and Sperisen shared a desire to establish a new approach to modern jewelry and began to work together to achieve innovative movement, spatial effects, and fluid transitions between metals and gems.

FIGURE 24
Margaret De Patta
Practice materials for gemstone cutting, c. 1939–64
acrylic and wood
¾ x ¾ x ¾ in.
(19 x 19 x 19 mm), average size
Margaret De Patta Archives,
Bielawski Trust,
Point Richmond, California

FIGURE 25
Margaret De Patta
Note to Francis Sperisen, c. 1946–60
graphite on paper
11 x 8½ in. (27.9 x 21.6 cm)
Margaret De Patta Archives,
Bielawski Trust,
Point Richmond, California

FIGURE 26
Margaret De Patta
Ring, 1946
sterling silver, tourmaline, quartz
1 x ¼ x ¼ in. (25 x 6 x 6 mm)
Collection of the Oakland Museum of California,
Gift of Eugene Bielawski,
The Margaret De Patta Memorial Collection

After De Patta returned to San Francisco from Chicago, their collaboration became increasingly inventive. De Patta created models of her designs, simulating crystalline effects by sawing, polishing, and drilling Lucite or balsa, and sent the models to Sperisen, who would cut facets in quartz to create the optical properties she sought (figs. 24, 25).[30] De Patta wanted to expand the traditional lapidary vocabulary beyond merely enhancing the brilliance of stones and collaborated with Sperisen to develop an ingenious method for creating what she called opticuts. In these gems the facets act as transparent windows allowing light to penetrate the stone and reveal its internal structure. An opticut might also magnify or refract light to alter the location and position of a jewelry component—such as the pin stem—so that it appears to move or change shape when worn. This lens effect, normally considered a fault in traditional gem cutting, was a radical departure, and the stunning visual effects raised De Patta's jewelry to a new level both in concept and in technical mastery. Sperisen and De Patta frequently manipulated the facets and inclusions in quartz crystal to create the sense of the eye traveling around corners into space, a process that allowed De Patta to explore illusion, transmission, occlusion, perspective, and spatial enhancement, often offsetting transparent and opaque surfaces. These opticuts were generally executed in rutilated quartz, which greatly heightened the internal optical effects (pl.17). De Patta also pioneered the use of quartz with tourmaline inclusions, exploiting the natural patterns in the stone to increase visual interest; when worn, the appearance of the stone changes with shifting light refractions (fig. 26).[31]

From the mid-1940s on, De Patta utilized an expanded palette of natural materials in her compositions, including coral, pearls, and malachite, to form a textural and natural counterpoint to the bare metal and stainless steel screens. She also introduced greater variations in color, shape, and rhythm, as in her pin in silver with malachite and jasper from around 1947 (fig. 27). Using an asymmetrical arrangement, she achieved a dynamic balance

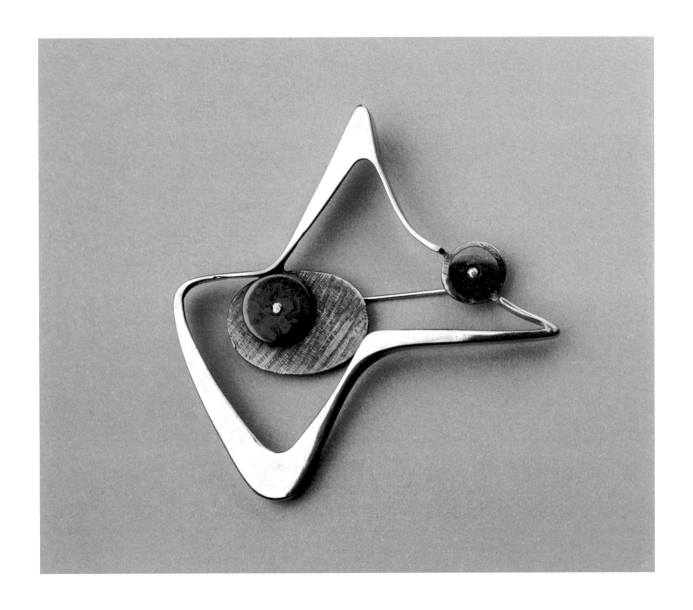

FIGURE 27
Margaret De Patta
Pin, c. 1947
sterling silver, malachite, jasper
2⅞ x 2⅞ in. (73 x 73 mm)
Montreal Museum of Fine Arts,
Liliane and David M. Stewart Collection

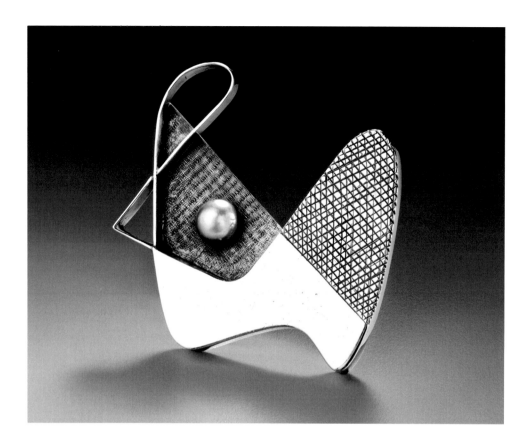

with changing line width and varied stone size and placement. While transparency remained a dominant theme in her work, she diversified her visual vocabulary by contrasting textured surfaces, as in her pin from around 1945 in which cross hatching is juxtaposed with highly polished silver and a black pearl set on darkened silver (fig. 28) and her pin from around 1949 in which sterling silver and a stainless steel mesh screen are layered, a type of piece she referred to as a tactile (fig. 29).

Moholy-Nagy famously advised De Patta, "Catch your stones in the air. Make them float in space. Don't enclose them."[32] In response, De Patta developed ingenious methods of attaching stones so that they appeared to obey Moholy-Nagy's dictate.

She discovered that backings could be invisible from the front of the design if she attached them to a blind spot in the stone created by the curvature of the cabochon. She also gave serious thought to her mountings, frequently structuring them architecturally to emphasize an asymmetrical composition with cantilevered components. Alternatively, she might conceal the supports, as in her sterling silver, quartz, and stainless steel pendant from 1950 (see p.67, fig. 14). In this piece De Patta used optical qualities that magnify and bend light through the cabochon quartz, effectively making the mount invisible. The opaque mesh screen behind the stone seems to float, yet provides a fixed reference point as movement and changing light transform the piece.

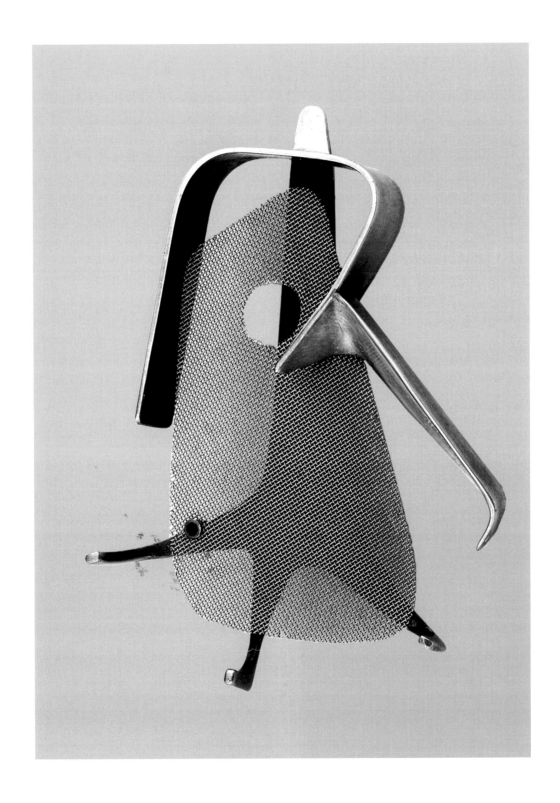

De Patta declared of her pieces, "It was my good fortune to come along historically at the opportune time to open up exploration in the visual properties of gem stones. Thus, it becomes possible to see entirely through some of the stones in my rings and other jewelry mountings."[33] In a 1948 pendant the asymmetric shape of the quartz crystal creates tension in relation to the diagonal lines of the rutile inclusions (a dark titanium dioxide mineral) (see p. 59, fig. 3). The two rectangular gold elements, one in front of the stone and the other behind it, create a visual ricochet that enhances the impact of the transmission of light through the quartz. Gold metalwork holds the stone in place only along one edge, and the entire piece is dynamically balanced like a Calder mobile, with the larger gold rectangle acting as a critical visual and physical counterweight.

As a balance to these demanding and time-consuming pieces, De Patta also made more casual "sweater jewelry," frequently designed around her vast collection of beach stones and pebbles, which she began using in the 1950s. De Patta wrote, "I felt different about pebbles than about other stones. They shouldn't be enclosed but should be free as they are in nature." To create the floating illusion perfected in a pin from around 1964, a late example, she used a diamond drill to make a slot in the stone, which was then filled with epoxy and attached to the metal element, leaving no visible means of support (see p.69, fig. 17). Because it was important to De Patta that her jewelry was durable, in her meticulous fashion, she undertook extensive testing of different epoxies before settling on a formula and heating technique to adhere the stones.

Although she created intriguing designs for pendants, rings, earrings and the occasional bracelet, the pin remained her dominant jewelry form; sterling silver her metal of choice; and, aside from quartz, such non-precious materials as amber, coral, malachite, onyx, and pearls her preferred components. De Patta often used moving components within her jewelry to

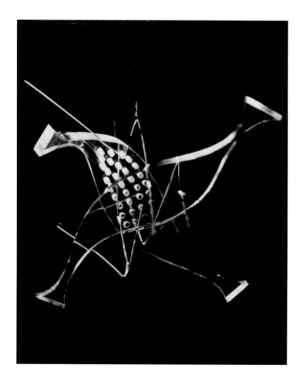

change a piece's appearance and even its shape by reversing positive and negative design elements. The textured, biomorphic shape in her pin from around 1947 to 1950 slides to alter its position in order to cover or reveal the stones on the recessed suspensions (see p. 62, fig.9). The effect is dramatized in her 1947 time-lapse photograph *Three Position Pin in Movement* (fig. 31), taken by De Patta and noted photographer Milton Halberstadt (1919–2000).[34] The kinetic pin is another example of De Patta's ability to use jewelry to realize Moholy-Nagy's theory of vision in motion, and the photograph bears a strong resemblance to his 1943 *Plexiglas Mobile Sculpture in Repose and in Motion* (fig. 30). While

not kinetic, her Mondrian-like pin from 1950 can be worn vertically or horizontally, and its red and white stones can be turned over to change color and alter perception (see p.70, fig. 18).[35]

One of the first jewelers to use the phrase *wearable sculpture*, De Patta took into account both human anatomy and movement and enjoyed working out intricate yet elegant solutions to locking mechanisms and clasps for earrings and pendants. She developed interlocking rings and ring shanks designed to conform to the actual contours of fingers, and while she experimented with moving components in some of her jewelry, in pieces such

FIGURE 30 [LEFT]
László Moholy-Nagy (1895–1946)
Plexiglas Mobile Sculpture in Repose and in Motion, 1943
gelatin silver prints
6⅝ x 4⅜ x in., 6½ x 4½ in. (16.8 x 11.1 cm, 16.5 x 11.4 cm)
Courtesy of George Eastman House, International Museum of
Photography and Film

FIGURE 31
Margaret De Patta and **Milton Halberstadt (1919–2000)**
Three Position Pin in Movement, 1947
multiple exposure, gelatin silver print,
6 x 8¾ in. (15.2 x 22.2 cm)
Collection of Leland Rice and Susan Ehrens

as her 1946 sterling silver ring (fig. 26) she was careful to prevent unwanted twisting so the presentation of the design would not change.

Demand Exceeds Supply, Late 1940s

By the mid-1940s, De Patta had gained widespread recognition for her unique pieces, but her process was meticulous and demanding. In order to justify the time spent on a single piece, she had to increase prices to more than $125 (more than $1,500 in constant dollars[36]). In an article for *Arts & Architecture* in 1947, she asked, "What happens to an artist when the demand for his work exceeds his ability to supply it? If he is realistic, he reaps the benefit of raising the price to the point where a temporary equilibrium is established between supply and demand. What then happens to this artist's work? It necessarily becomes the possession of the very few who are in a position to pay these luxury prices. This is the situation I found myself in—a multitude of friends of my work who were unable to own and enjoy it."[37] Such exclusivity represented a breach of the democratic Bauhaus principles both she and her husband staunchly supported.

Because De Patta wanted to make a meaningful contribution to society and because she believed that modern production methods had the potential to turn out fine articles at lower cost, she was determined to emulate Bauhaus success in bridging the gap between individual craftsmanship and production. There is no doubt that Eugene Bielawski had a major influence in this respect. In October 1946, the couple started making limited edition production pieces in their San Francisco home studio, later calling their company Designs Contemporary.

De Patta and Bielawski undertook all of the arduous and demanding functions from production management to advertising and packaging, with the longtime goal of achieving enough sales that the artist would "re-emerge shorn of his traditional impracticality."[38] De Patta designed between forty and fifty master models in silver, which were cast by Bielawski only when they received an order because they could not afford to tie up funds in inventory. One such piece, a pin she designed in 1949 (fig. 32), remained in production until 1957. Crafted in silver with mesh and metal elements, and with an overall design that utilizes reproducible biomorphic shapes within a Constructivist composition, the piece bears a strong resemblance to an untitled photogram (fig. 33), suggesting that she continued to find such images of value in translating two-dimensional images into three-dimensional jewelry.

De Patta stated confidently that the Designs Contemporary production pieces were comparable in both material and workmanship to her individually handcrafted one-of-a-kind pieces and expressed delight when collectors said they were unable to tell the difference between the unique and the serially produced pieces. As evidence of this conviction, in 1946 when she sent work to the groundbreaking Museum of Modern Art exhibition *Modern Handcrafted Jewelry,* she made sure that both one-of-a-kind pieces and serial jewelry were represented. While it is true that a higher end production piece such as her silver and quartz pin designed in 1946 (fig. 34) compares well with her 1945 pin (fig. 28), other production pieces were clearly less intricate in design, such as the sterling silver pin in production from 1946 to 1957 (fig. 35). All serially produced pieces were the result of lost-wax casting and lacked the detail and precision of De Patta's unique pieces, which she never cast, strongly preferring to work the metal by hand.

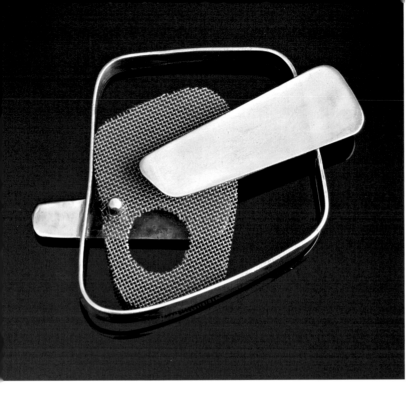

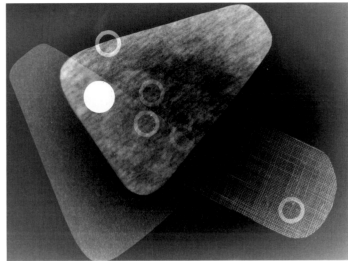

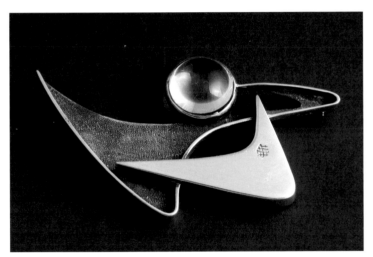

FIGURE 32 [UPPER LEFT]

Margaret De Patta

Production Pin #41

designed 1949, produced 1949–57

sterling silver, stainless steel screen

2¾ x 3⅛ x ⅝ in. (70 x 79 x 16 mm)

Private collection

FIGURE 33 [UPPER RIGHT]

Margaret De Patta

Untitled photogram, 1939

gelatin silver print

7¼ x 9⅞ in. (18.4 x 25 cm)

Collection of Leland Rice and Susan Ehrens

FIGURE 34

Margaret De Patta

Production Pin #6,

designed 1946, produced 1946–57

sterling silver, quartz

2 x 3½ x ½ in. (51 x 89 x 13 mm)

Private collection

FIGURE 35

Margaret De Patta

Production Pin #4,

designed 1944, produced 1946–57

sterling silver

¾ x 1 x ¾ in. (19 x 25 x 19 mm)

Collection of the Oakland Museum of California,

Gift of Eugene Bielawski, The Margaret De Patta

Memorial Collection

In contrast to the elite 1946 MoMA exhibition—which displayed De Patta's jewelry alongside works by Pablo Picasso, Jean Arp, and Alexander Calder— the Walker Art Center's exhibition in Minneapolis, Minnesota, two years later, *Modern Jewelry Under Fifty Dollars,* brought De Patta together with thirty-one other artist/jewelers. This show emphasized the importance of jewelry not for its traditional monetary or status value but for its ability to enhance the wearer's appearance and for its artistic value.[39] De Patta described the Walker Art Center's Everyday Art Gallery as "an outstanding example of the value of constant displays of the best designed mass-produced articles of everyday use."[40]

Teaching and The Metal Arts Guild

Influenced by Moholy-Nagy's emphasis on the importance of education, De Patta strove to teach during the 1940s and 1950s, even as she advanced her own study. Her most significant experience was at the Tom Mooney Labor School (later

renamed the California Labor School), which opened in San Francisco in August 1942, during the war. The school's motto was "Education for Victory," and its program promised to analyze social, economic, and political questions in light of the struggle against fascism around the world. Its mission was to support education for San Francisco workers and to improve the lives of working adults throughout the Bay Area, with classes offered in language skills, history, art, and theater, as well as union organizing (fig. 36).

De Patta began teaching in the art and crafts department in 1944 under a program designed to help students test "by means of experimentation and construction, the aesthetic and physical qualities and the functional possibilities of all kinds of materials, whether applied to a painting, the designing of useful objects, or to a housing project."[41] In the summer of 1946, industrial arts training was added to attract returning veterans with GI Bill of Rights funding, and Eugene Bielawski became director of the program. Under his guidance, the teaching methods closely paralleled those of the Chicago Bauhaus, emphasizing experi-

FIGURE 36
California Labor School course catalogues for 1944, 1945, and 1948
Margaret De Patta Archives, Bielawski Trust, Point Richmond, California

menting with materials and solving practical problems.[42] Workshops in basic design, metal, and photography, and classes in graphic arts, drawing, social science, economics, and labor issues, were intended to give students an understanding of the relationship between modern industrial art and current society.

Over her four-year affiliation with the school, De Patta maintained a demanding teaching schedule that included responsibility for such courses as Modern Design for Small Crafts, Experimental Stage Designs, Basic Design Workshop, Plastics, Sculpture, and Home Planning on a Shoestring, a class she conducted with Bielawski.[43] In the basic design workshop, which she taught each year, students designed and then used hand and power tools to produce useful objects in a variety of materials, including wood, plastic, and metal.

In 1946, the political climate of the McCarthy era intensified, and the California Senate Fact-Finding Committee on Un-American Activities (SUAC) investigated the school. The school was accused of being Communist-sponsored despite its ownership by the

California Labor School and the University of California. De Patta and Bielawski left in 1947, but they were blacklisted from 1947 through 1949 in reports published by the California State Senate and felt as if they were being persecuted for the ideals in which they believed.[44] The school was forced to close in 1957.[45]

No longer able to teach Bauhaus-inspired design concepts at the California Labor School, the Bielawskis purchased thirty acres of land in Napa County in 1946 with the intention of establishing an artists' cooperative school of contemporary design. This plan, however, never came to fruition. In 1951 the couple purchased a farmhouse in the Napa Valley and spent more than five years turning it into a modern home reflecting their keen interest in modern architecture and interior design. Their modernist taste and philosophy aimed for functionality, and they used unusual materials and structural elements to change the appearance of the house. When the ceiling proved too low for remodeling, they added vertical accent lines to the interior walls and installed a forty-foot long floor-to-ceiling window in the living room and a wide expanse of translucent screen barred with strong verticals

FIGURE 37
Napa Valley house after renovation, c. 1958
Margaret De Patta Archives, Bielawski Trust,
Point Richmond, California

FIGURE 38
Napa Valley house after renovation, c. 1958
Margaret De Patta Archives, Bielawski Trust,
Point Richmond, California

to give the illusion of height (fig. 37). To unify the appearance, they clad the exterior of the house in narrow vertical redwood panels (fig. 38).[46]

Just as she integrated the mounts of her jewelry into her design, De Patta devised a floor-to-ceiling bookcase with a lattice ladder of two-inch iron pipe to create a solution for reaching books on the top shelves that was both decorative and functional. Her unique dining table was constructed of terrazzo with built-in plates consisting of depressions in the tabletop (see p.138, fig. 16); side dishes and glasses fit into a removable cork mat, and a small asbestos-lined brazier in the center of the table kept food and beverages warm. Reflecting her love of natural stones, the coffee table was surfaced with smooth pebbles set in cement.[47]

From the late 1940s to the early 1950s, De Patta and Bielawski frequently hosted informal gatherings of artists and craftsmen for the purpose of discussing metalsmithing and more generally the state of craft and design at mid-century. The Metal Arts Guild, which De Patta and Bielawski helped to establish in 1951 in San Francisco, grew out of these casual get-togethers.[48] The other founders of the guild included jewelers Peter Macchiarini, Irena Brynner, Harry Dixon, Merry Renk, Caroline Rosene, Bob Winston, and several colleagues from their California Labor School days. De Patta took an early leadership role as president of the Guild from 1955 to 1956.

The mission of the Metal Arts Guild was "to bring together the Metal Artists and Craftsmen of the Bay Area in an association for their mutual development, strength and advantage." When the Guild met each month, craftsmen exchanged information about methods, standards of design, materials, equipment sources, outlets, and pricing. The Guild helped to unify and promote the northern California jewelry community, with members regularly exhibiting together, and brought the region's artists both national and international recognition. Jeweler Irena Brynner described the Metal Arts Guild as "one of the most satisfying and successful craft organizations I ever belonged to."[49]

De Patta was also a panelist at the first American Craft Council national conference held at Asilomar, California, in 1957, a landmark event. At the second national conference in 1958 in Lake Geneva, Wisconsin, she was a panelist for *Vision and Individual Response,* a seminar in which she described the core elements of her work: "freedom to develop or use new materials, freedom to manipulate materials by newly developed techniques, and the necessity to incorporate the influences of our time."[50] Through her desire to share her views on design, production, and the role of education, she began work on a book of design to outline "historical influences on the artist, the development of jewelry design, and . . . a general evaluation in all creative fields.[51] Papers from her estate contain notes and outlines for articles and essays, as well as a preface for the unpublished book.

FIGURE 39
Margaret De Patta
Schematic drawing of pressure points for knife from International Design Competion entry, 1960
mixed media
6½ x 13 in. (16.5 x 33 cm)
Margaret De Patta Archives, Bielawski Trust, Point Richmond, California

FIGURE 40
Margaret De Patta
Wooden prototypes for flatware, 1959
wood and acrylic paint
fork: 1¼ x 7 x 1¼ in. (3.2 x 17.8 x 3.2 cm);
knife: 1 x 8¾ x 1 in. (2.5 x 22.2 x 2.5 cm);
spoon: 1 x 6⅜ x 1⅜ in. (2.5 x 16.2 x 3.4 cm)
Margaret De Patta Archives, Bielawski Trust, Point Richmond, California

Experiments in Production Work

Throughout her career De Patta maintained a belief in the validity of production work and accepted a modest number of assignments in other media including ceramics. One of her earliest commissions was from a costume jewelry company in the late 1940s, for which she assembled very simple earrings into twenty-five different designs, using an assortment of machine-punched parts. While the earrings were priced at just one or two dollars, they never found a market because their avant-garde style proved too great a departure from the traditional jewelry that buyers were accustomed to purchasing (see p.123, fig. 24).[52] Once again, De Patta found herself at odds with the public she sought to design for.

Despite the fact that Designs Contemporary was selling her production jewelry to galleries in New York City and San Francisco, as well as to outlets throughout the country,[53] the firm was not a financial success,[54] and De Patta continued to struggle. One can only speculate that the continued pressures to make ends meet undermined her conviction that she could replicate the success of the Bauhaus in reconciling social and political philosophies with commercial realities.

With the failure of her innovative two-dollar earrings, De Patta was frustrated by her inability to change consumers' ingrained buying patterns. She stated, "The Purchaser's taste is conditioned by the choice between one conventional design and another just as bad."[55] She had made an enormous personal investment in the production of less expensive pieces for a larger, but anonymous clientele, yet these works failed to gain wide acceptance. Once again, she must have been disappointed that the democratic principles on which she had based her life and work had not produced the envisioned results.

Despite her lack of success with modestly priced pieces, De Patta's exacting one-of-a-kind pieces from this time demonstrate increasing innovation and skill. Her carefully integrated design for a 1959 pendant features rays of white gold forming a mount for a complex faceted opticut rhomboid quartz crystal (pl. 1). The ebony and white-gold elements placed behind the stone appear as multiple images. The piece is a very fine example of her

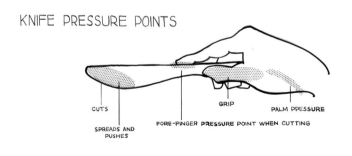

KNIFE PRESSURE POINTS

CUTS
GRIP
PALM PPESSURE
SPREADS AND PUSHES
FORE-FINGER PRESSURE POINT WHEN CUTTING

PROBLEM   TO INTEGRATE PRESSURE POINTS INTO FUNCTIONAL AND AESTHETIC ENTITY

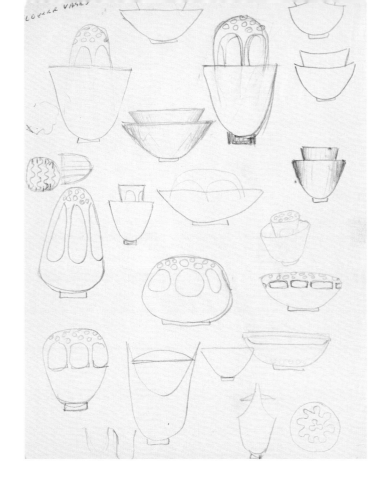

FIGURE 41
Margaret De Patta
Salt and pepper shakers, c. 1960
ceramic
2¾ x 2¾ x 2⅞ in. (7 x 7 x 7.3 cm), each
Margaret De Patta Archives, Bielawski Trust,
Point Richmond, California

FIGURE 42
Margaret De Patta
Flower vases, c. 1960
ceramic
large vase: 6 x 4¾ x 4½ in. (15.2 x 12.1 x 11.4 cm);
small vase: 4 x 4⅝ x 4½ in. (10.2 x 11.8 x 11.4 cm)
Margaret De Patta Archives, Bielawski Trust,
Point Richmond, California

mature work, in which the effect of light and movement change the piece through the refractive quality of the facets on the stone.[56]

De Patta also turned her attention to designing cutlery (fig. 40). In 1960 she won a five-hundred-dollar grant to design flatware for the International Design Competition for Sterling Silver Flatware (fig. 39). When her design was eliminated in the second round, she noted, "The trouble was that I didn't realize we already have a modern tradition. We're stylized—with extreme simplification of forms. . . . I started out with a form that would be good in the hand—a form functional and satisfying to hold."[57]

FIGURE 43
Margaret De Patta
Sketches for flower vases, 1959
graphite on paper
10 x 8½ in. (25.4 x 21.6 cm)
Margaret De Patta Archives, Bielawski Trust,
Point Richmond, California

Although her design was eliminated and never went into production, her flatware was featured at the Georg Jensen *Vision* exhibition in New York City in 1960.

De Patta's most unusual production design commission came from one of her former California Labor School colleagues, ceramist Edith Kiertzner Heath (1911–2005). In 1959 De Patta took time off from jewelry making to develop designs for Heath Ceramics in Sausalito, California.[58] She used this opportunity to further explore ways to combine beauty and function. She observed, "I hate to turn a pitcher around every time I want to pass it. Why not have multiple handles and spouts to provide complete freedom in handling and pouring?"[59] Shunning traditional wheel-thrown forms, she created such functional pieces as salt and pepper shakers (fig. 41), a container for fat drippings, dinnerware, and vases (fig. 42). Unfortunately, Heath did not produce her designs because it would have necessitated constructing an entire line in order to sell the pieces as a group.[60]

1960–1964 and Legacy

By the 1960s, De Patta was only working on commissions or experimenting with new design solutions for her unique pieces of jewelry. Due to her reputation, special orders came in from all over the country. Believing that jewelry should express an individual's taste and ideas, she sent out a questionnaire with eight questions regarding the purpose of the piece, the preferred metal and stones, the general size and intended purpose, and whether it should be open, massive, or delicate. The design itself, how-

FIGURE 44
Margaret De Patta
Necklet, 1961
14K white gold, quartz, diamonds
1 x 6 in. (25 x 150 mm)
Goldsmiths' Hall, London

ever, was her prerogative alone, and once a design was created for a specific customer, she never repeated it without the owner's permission since she felt that a design belonged exclusively to the individual who commissioned it.[61]

De Patta's exhibition record tells the story of both her rising artistic reputation and the kinds of venues where the work of emerging modern studio craft artisans was welcomed and promoted. De Patta participated in exhibitions throughout California, ranging from craft fairs to commercial galleries and major exhibitions such as *Jewelry, Past and Present* in 1957 at the Long Beach Museum of Art. When the Museum of Contemporary Crafts (now the Museum of Arts and Design) in New York launched its inaugural exhibition, *Craftsmanship in a Changing World,* in 1956, De Patta's jewelry was among the nearly two hundred craft objects on display. Two years later the American Craft Council organized the American craft entries for the U.S.

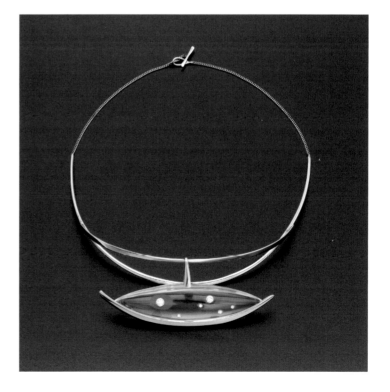

Pavilion at the Brussels World's Fair and the jewelry section included pieces by De Patta, Irena Brynner, John Paul Miller, Ruth and Svetozar Radakovich, Christian Schmidt, and Robert Von Neumann.[62]

In 1961, the Worshipful Company of Goldsmiths sponsored the *International Exhibition of Modern Jewellery, 1890–1961* in association with the Victoria and Albert Museum in London. De Patta, one of only five Americans whose work was chosen for the exhibition, was represented by a quartz necklet with diamonds (fig. 44) that was shown alongside pieces by Pablo Picasso, Alexander Calder, and such renowned jewelry houses as Lalique, Tiffany, and Cartier. Goldsmiths' Hall later bought the necklet for its collection. The placement of diamonds within transparent quartz is similar to that in a pendant that was shown at the Brussels World's Fair in 1958 and also resembles a 1960 pendant with white gold, quartz, and five inlaid diamonds (pl. 22). In these

three pieces, unusual for their incorporation of precious stones, De Patta overturned the traditional hierarchy of materials, employing diamonds not for their intrinsic value but for their reflective and color qualities.

From October 1960 to January 1961, De Patta and Bielawski shared a joyous trip to Japan and Hong Kong, seeing Buddhist temples, visiting the studios of craft artisans, and spending time with a friend who taught there. They stayed in local inns, and De Patta's letters to friends and family document a leisurely and fun-filled vacation. They were particularly surprised and delighted by the attention of the Japanese school children and constantly took their pictures (fig. 45).[63]

After her return, however, De Patta's letters took an alarming tone as she frequently referred to plaguing financial problems exacerbated by the failure to sell their Napa Valley house even after they had moved into more frugal living quarters in Oakland.[64] The innovations De Patta had proudly built into the house were probably too avant-garde for many buyers and may have contributed to keeping it on the market for over two years, which further increased the frustration.

In the early 1960s, De Patta's depression seemed to deepen around a marital crisis as Bielawski suffered from a loss of purpose and direction.[65] His dejection, which may have been related to the decision to close their production company, weighed on her, as did hints that he was jealous of her artistic recognition. The rampant change in cultural expressions and stylistic preferences during this period—the ironic, confrontational, and derisive attitudes that animated emerging art movements in the 1960s and challenged the cool, rational approach of modernist design on which she had built her career—may have contributed to her dispiritedness. She produced little work during these years, and as the foundation on which she had built her existence crumbled, she succumbed to a sense of hopelessness and profound anguish. On March 19, 1964, the day after her sixty-first birthday, she took her own life.

In the year of Margaret De Patta's untimely death, her artistic reputation was secured in national and international arenas based on a body of work reflecting Constructivist principles and the Bauhaus tenets that had informed them. Within months of her passing, her friends mounted the *Margaret De Patta Memorial Exhibition* at the San Francisco Museum of Art from collections loaned by Bielawski. Giacomo Patri, a colleague at the California Labor School and fellow member of the Metal Arts Guild said, "She revolutionized the concept of jewelry-making. For centuries, jewelry had reproduced natural forms like birds, fish and

people. And it had been centered around precious stones. But the trend away from this was heavily influenced by her, both here and in Europe.[66]

Throughout her life, Margaret De Patta expressed her conviction that an artist's work should reflect the age in which it is created, that designs should be well conceived, that the integrity of materials should never be violated, and that jewelry should be made with the individual in mind. Well-designed jewelry, De Patta wrote, "must be comfortable to the wearer in respect to size, weight and durability. It must characterize our times, just as good design in any field must reflect the materials, techniques, and concepts of our own day."[67]

Margaret De Patta's exquisitely balanced compositions captured the essence of modernist design, but her legacy extends far beyond her ability to reflect the materials, techniques, and concepts of her own day. By liberating jewelry from reliance on traditional forms and materials and by setting extremely high standards for conceptual brilliance and technical mastery, she helped establish the foundation on which contemporary jewelry developed and on which it continues to evolve today.

1

Yoshiko Uchida, "Margaret De Patta," in *The Jewelry of Margaret De Patta: A Retrospective Exposition,* February 3–March 28, 1976, ed. Hazel Bray (Oakland, Calif.: The Oakland Museum, 1976), 15.

2

Peter Selz, "The Impact from Abroad: Foreign Guests and Visitors," in *On the Edge of America: California Modernist Art 1900–1950,* ed. Paul J. Karlstrom (Berkeley and Los Angeles: University of California Press, 1996), 98.

3

Ibid. 102. The Oakland Art Gallery (now part of the Oakland Museum of California) opened in 1915; the California Palace of the Legion of Honor opened in 1924; and the Mills College Art Gallery (now the Mills College Art Museum) in Oakland opened in 1925. German émigré Galka Scheyer was an apostle of modern art and organized such exhibitions as *European Modernists* in 1929 at the Oakland Art Gallery. She was an ardent supporter of the work of the Blue Four: Wassily Kandinsky, Alexei Jawlensky, Lyonel Feininger, and Paul Klee.

4

Robert Cardinale and Hazel Bray, "Margaret De Patta: Structure Concepts and Design Sources," *Metalsmith* 3, no. 2 (spring 1983): 11.

5

This was De Patta's third marriage. Her first husband died of tuberculosis, and a brief second marriage ended in divorce.

6

Helen Civelli, "Wedding Ring Starts Girl on Career," *San Francisco News,* 2 January 1940, 7.

7

"Jewels in Modern Setting: Margaret de Patta Creates a Challenge," *California Arts & Architecture* 57, no. 9 (September 1940): 18; Cardinale and Bray, "Margaret De Patta," 11–12.

8

Toni Lesser Wolf, Introduction to *Masterworks of Contemporary American Jewelry: Sources and Concepts* (London: Victoria and Albert Museum, 1985), 8; Toni Greenbaum and Pat Kirkham, "Women Jewelry Designers," in *Women Designers in the USA, 1900–2000: Diversity and Difference,* ed. Pat Kirkham (New Haven, Conn.: Yale University Press, 2000), 204.

9

Civelli, "Wedding Ring Starts Girl on Career," 7.

10

Ibid.

11

Margaret De Patta Bielawski, "From the Inside," *The Palette* 32, no. 2 (spring 1952): 15.

12

Margaret De Patta, "De Patta," *Design Quarterly* 33 (1955): 6.

13

The other exhibitions included the California Pacific International Exposition in San Diego in 1935–36 and a series at Amberg-Hirth Gallery, the noted San Francisco craft gallery, in the late 1930s. Cardinale and Bray, "Margaret De Patta," 12; Uchida, "Margaret De Patta," 8; "April Exhibitions in Local Galleries," *San Francisco Art Association Bulletin* 2, no 11 (April 1936): 8.

14

For an excellent overview of the various stylistic influences prevalent in the California art scene during that time, see Karlstrom, ed., *On the Edge of America: California Modernist Art, 1900–1950* (Berkeley: University of California Press, 1996).

15

László Molohy-Nagy's lecture was published as "The Bauhaus Education," in *Proceedings of the Pacific Arts Association, Fourteenth Annual Convention, San Francisco, April 1–4, 1939,* 59–68. My sincere thanks to Leland Rice and Susan Ehrens for bringing this important publication to my attention.

16

Avant-garde artists in Russia coined the term *Constructivism* in the early 1920s for paintings, sculpture, architecture, and design together with developments in photography, film, literature, and theater. Also called production art because its goal was to create artist-engineers who would revolutionize industrial design, the movement rapidly achieved wide international currency.

17

Joseph H. Caton, *The Utopian Vision of Moholy-Nagy* (Ann Arbor, Michigan: UMI Research Press, 1984), 13.

18

László Moholy-Nagy, "Constructivism and the Proletariat," in *Moholy-Nagy, An Anthology,* ed. Richard Kostelanetz (Cambridge, Mass.: Da Capo Press, 1970), 185–86.

19

Moholy-Nagy, "Constructivism and the Proletariat," 59.

20

Emanuel Mervir Benson, "The Chicago Bauhaus and Moholy-Nagy," *Magazine of Art* 31 (1938), 83.

21

Moholy-Nagy, "Constructivism and the Proletariat," 59.

22

Ibid.

23

De Patta Bielawski, "From the Inside," 17.

24

Margaret De Patta's personal travel journal (What We Saw), 1939, Margaret De Patta Archives, Bielawski Trust, Point Richmond, California.

25

Selz, "The Impact from Abroad," 112.

26

Uchida, "Margaret De Patta," 14.

27

Eugene Bielawski, "Margaret De Patta—An Analysis of Her Work in Jewelry," in *The Jewelry of Margaret De Patta: A Retrospective Exposition, February 3–March 28, 1976,* ed. Hazel Bray (Oakland, Calif.: The Oakland Museum, 1976), 28.

28

Susan Landauer, "Painting under the Shadow: California Modernism and the Second World War," in Karlstrom, ed., *On the Edge of America,* 428.

29

From 1919 to 1923 Sperisen worked as an apprentice at Moser Brothers in San Francisco studying the art of faceting, before opening his own shop. See Judy Frosh, "Francis Sperisen: Master Lapidary," *American Craft* 45, no. 1 (February–March 1985): 40, 41; Richard W. Wise, "Secrets of the Gem Trade: Margaret De Patta and the American Lapidary Renaissance," *Modern Silver* (2003), online at http://www.modernsilver.com/secretsofthegemtrade.htm (accessed 20 October 2011).

30

Cardinale and Bray, "Margaret De Patta," 13.

31

Jane Ro, "Margaret De Patta: Floating Stones," *American Society of Jewelry Historians Newsletter* 24, no. 3 (winter 2010): 3–6.

32

Uchida, "Margaret De Patta," 15.

33

Bernice Stevens Decker, "Couple Make Sculptured Jewelry," *Christian Science Monitor,* 24 November 1958, 10P.

34

"Jewels in Modern Setting: Margaret de Patta Creates a Challenge," *California Arts & Architecture* 57, no. 9 (September 1940): 18.

35

In 1924, Moholy-Nagy dedicated a Bauhaus publication to Mondrian: László Moholy-Nagy, "Piet Mondrian: Neue Gestaltung," *Bauhausbücher* 5 (Munich: Albert Langen Verlag, 1924).

36

"Constant dollars" refers here to the value of the dollar in 2011.

37
Margaret De Patta, "De Patta," *Arts & Architecture* 64, no. 7 (July 1947): 30.

38
Uchida, "Margaret De Patta," 17.

39
"Modern Jewelry under Fifty Dollars," *Everyday Art Quarterly* 7 (spring 1948): 6.

40
Margaret De Patta, "Behind the Scenes with the Craftsman," unpublished manuscript, c. 1950. Margaret De Patta Archives, Bielawski Trust, Point Richmond, California.

41
California Labor School Catalogue, Summer, 1944, California Labor School Collection, 1942–1957, Labor Archive and Research Center, San Francisco State University, San Francisco, Calif.

42
New Opportunities in Industrial Arts, brochure, California Labor School Collection, 1942–1957, Labor Archive and Research Center, San Francisco State University, San Francisco, Calif.

43
California Labor School Catalogues, Winter/Spring, 1944; Summer, 1944; Spring, 1945; Fall, 1945; Winter, 1945; Spring, 1946; Fall, 1946; Spring, 1947; California Labor School Collection, 1942–1957, Labor Archive and Research Center, San Francisco State University, San Francisco, Calif.

44
California Legislature, Senate. *Index Un-American Activities in California, For Reports of 1943, 1945, 1947, 1948, 1949, 1951* [Sacramento]: Senate of the State of California, [1951]; Description for the Inventory of the California Labor School Collection, 1942–1957, Online Archive of California, Labor Archive and Research Center, San Francisco State University, San Francisco, Calif: http://www.oac.cdlib.org/findaid/ark:/13030/tf0489n414/ (accessed 27 September 2010).

45
Unfortunately, the school's troubles did not stop. Despite its earlier successes, the California Labor School lost its state accreditation in 1948 because many of the founding members were involved in union activities deemed Communist. Although President Holland Roberts fought to keep the school open, it continued to lose influence. That same year the school was also cited as a subversive and Communist organization in San Francisco by President Harry S. Truman's Attorney General Tom Clark. These charges plagued the school for the next nine years, and in 1957 the Subversive Activities Control Board required the school to register as a Communist front. This final blow, coupled with the reversal of the school's tax-exempt status—creating a tax bill that was impossible to pay back—forced the school to cease operations.

46
Anonymous, "Farmhouse Turned into Modern Home," *Napa Register*, 26 January 1957, 11-A.

47
Ibid.

48
A discussion of the founding of the Metal Arts Guild is found in Toni Greenbaum, "Constructivism and American Studio Jewelry, 1940 to the Present," *Studies in the Decorative Arts* 6, no. 1 (fall-winter 1998–99), 78-79.

49
Irena Brynner, *Jewelry As an Art Form* (New York: Van Nostrand Reinhold, 1979), 22.

50
Margaret De Patta, "Vision and Individual Response," transcript, quoted in Marcia Manhart, Tom Manhart, and Carol Haralson, *The Eloquent Object: The Evolution of American Art in Craft Media since 1945* (Tulsa, Okla.: The Philbrook Museum of Art, 1987), 16.

51
Uchida, "Margaret De Patta," 23.

52
Ibid., 19.

53
"Work of Margaret De Patta, Genius of Modern Jewelry Design, to be Shown Here," *Press Democrat,* 6 November 1949; Frankie Teague Childers, "Napa Woman Turns Hobby of Handsome Jewelry into Thriving Business in Stores Throughout U.S.," *Napa Register,* 9 July 1954.

54
See Julie M. Muñiz, "Jewelry for a Never-Increasing Minority: Margaret De Patta in the Market Place," in this volume.

55
Margaret De Patta, "De Patta," *Arts & Architecture 64*, no. 7 (July 1947): 30.

56
Ro, "Floating Stones," 3-4.

57
International Silverware Competition letter, Margaret De Patta Archives, Bielawski Trust, Point Richmond, California.

58
Uchida, "Margaret De Patta," 20.

59
Ibid.

60
For a good overview of Heath Ceramics and its tableware production, see Amos Klausner, *Heath Ceramics: The Complexity of Simplicity* (San Francisco: Chronicle Books, 2006).

61
Uchida, "Margaret De Patta," 21.

62
"Brussels World Fair," *Craft Horizons* 18, no. 2 (March–April 1958): 47.

63
Margaret De Patta to friends and family, dated and undated letters, 17 October 1960, 22 October 1960, 28 October 1960, 1 November 1960, 9 November 1960, 19 November 1960, and 2 December 1960, Margaret De Patta Archives, Bielawski Trust, Point Richmond, California.

64
Adelyne Cross to Margaret De Patta, 16 August 1963, Margaret De Patta Archives, Bielawski Trust, Point Richmond, California.

65
See letters from Adelyne Cross to Margaret De Patta, 15 August 1961, and from Nedda Rosen to Margaret De Patta, 31 October 1961, Margaret De Patta Archives, Bielawski Trust, Point Richmond, California.

66
"Margaret De Patta Memorial Exhibition," *San Francisco Chronicle,* 22 July 1964.

67
Thomas B. Robertson, "Talk on Jewelry Slated at Gallery," *San Diego Union,* 4 November 1951.

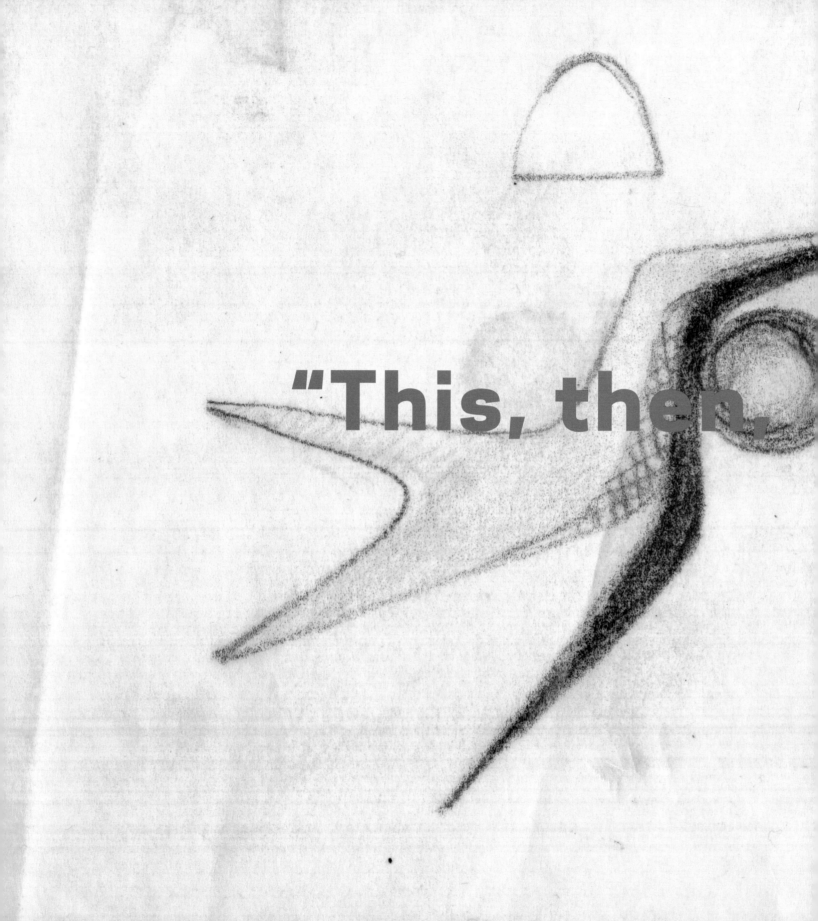

"This, then,

is the direction."

Silver - Black Epo...
Crystal

35 º º

Balancing Act
Margaret De Patta and Constructivism

GLENN ADAMSON

"This, then, is the direction." So wrote Margaret De Patta in the preface to her planned-for, but never published, book on modern design.[1] She was referring to the principles of Constructivism, which had their foundations in the art of revolutionary Russia, passed through the workshops of the Bauhaus in Germany, and were transmitted across the Atlantic in the heads and hands of artists fleeing the Nazis. Constructivism was a movement and a style, but above all it was a method. Its animating principle was to "rationalize artistic labor."[2] This meant that forms should arise from the technical exploration of structure and material. An artist's or designer's job is "constructive" in that it deals with the juxtaposition of qualities such as hardness, color, texture, elasticity, and facture (the marks imparted through making), all in response to a particular functional demand.

As this didactic concept of art making immediately suggests, Constructivism was very much a pedagogical phenomenon. Several of its progenitors—the photographer and graphic designer Alexander Rodchenko, the painters El Lissitzky and Kazimir Malevich, the sculptor Anton Pevsner, the designers Varvara Stepanova and Lyubov Popova, and the architect Vladimir Tatlin—taught at the VKhUTEMAS (an acronym in Russian for Higher Artistic and Technical Workshops), an experimental design school founded in 1920. This experimental Soviet institution warrants close comparison with the Bauhaus, where Constructivist principles were also extensively adopted. (El Lissitzky, who came to Germany in 1921, was an important conduit between the two institutions.) At both VKhUTEMAS and the Bauhaus, students were taught not about materials, but through them. They were set problem-solving tasks as a spur to wide-ranging creativity. Students might be asked to create sculpture from a sheet of paper with nothing but a pair of scissors (fig. 1), carve out a dynamic volume within a block of wood, or shear an organic form out of a rectangle of aluminum without removing any of the metal.[3]

The teaching methods of the Bauhaus were brought to America by Josef and Anni Albers, who moved to Black Mountain College in North Carolina in 1933, and by Lázsló Moholy-Nagy, a Hungarian polymath who moved fluidly between the fields of painting, sculpture, photography, film, typography, and design. Moholy-Nagy had only indirect experience of the Russian Constructivist experiment, but he adopted similar principles, looking for an "elemental art that does not philosophize, because it builds up its products from elements of its own."[4] One of several artists to flee the Bauhaus during its harrowing last days, he came to Chicago

in 1937, and there started a "New Bauhaus" in the former mansion of Marshall Field. Though the school folded after only a year, he went on to found the School of Design in Chicago, which eventually became the Institute of Design (it is now a part of the Illinois Institute of Technology). De Patta studied there with Moholy-Nagy in 1940–41. The annotated photographs that she took of her own work during her studies at the School of Design show her responding to set problems in the Constructivist mode. Some of the tasks were technical in nature ("hold stone without bezel"), while others were more evocative ("create forms for tactile identification and pleasure").[5]

Moholy-Nagy imparted design principles not only through such assignments but also through his aphoristic teaching. The advice of his that De Patta quoted most often, "catch your stones in air, make them float in space,"[6] was premised on the Constructivist principle of autonomous abstraction, by which a painting or object was created as a self-enclosed world of form. De Patta constantly experimented with setting stones in such a way as to make them levitate within a composition. Her "opticut" jewels and chunks of faceted quartz, in which stones were cut so as to produce an elusive, refractory effect, were a particularly ingenious means of achieving an impression of compositional autonomy. Like Moholy-Nagy's own *Light-Space Modulator,* which used reflection and illumination to destroy a stable impression of volume (fig. 2), her geometrically cut jewels seemed to contain an infinite number of visual possibilities (fig. 3). As this comparison suggests, Moholy-Nagy taught De Patta not only through pedagogical exercises but also by the example of his own polymorphous work. De Patta could not have failed to be impressed by his many experiments with time-based media, including kinetic sculptures, film, and light projection. For him Constructivism inhabited a temporal as

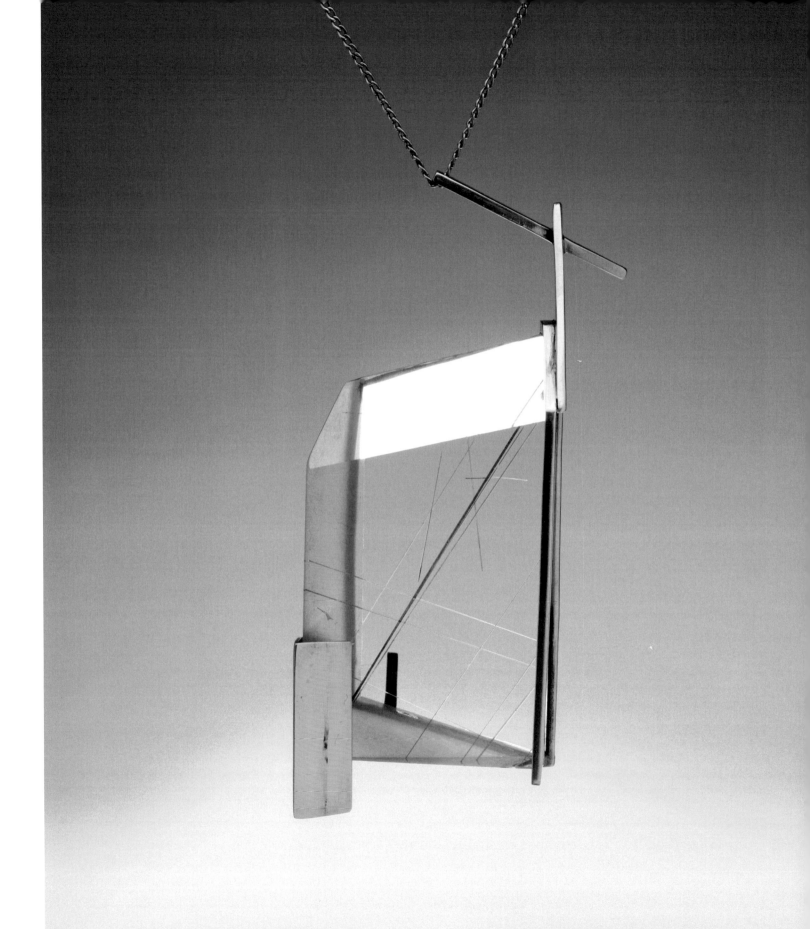

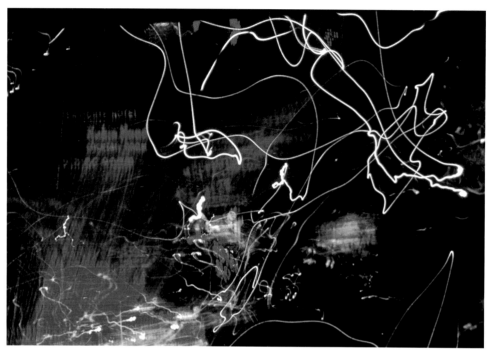

well as a spatial dimension. De Patta was thus encouraged to include moving elements in her jewelry and also to consider the importance of the body as a moving platform for her work.

Similarly, she drew lessons from Moholy-Nagy's use of photography, particularly a series of images in which he employed the camera as an automatic drawing device. By leaving the shutter open and jiggling the lens, he turned city views into dynamic compositions of looping lines and smeared signage (fig. 4). He also exploited the way that photography could collapse an open three-dimensional form into a complex but compacted two-

dimensional image, as in an extraordinary picture of timbers and rope that he made in 1940 (fig. 5). Though the loose construction anticipates the sculptural experiments of Robert Morris and Eva Hesse some three decades later, Moholy-Nagy seems to have intended it only as a prop—a way to get the quality of abstract drawing into a photo.

De Patta made images based on both of these principles (fig. 6), and she also experimented with Moholy-Nagy's photogram technique (used, as well, by other modernist photographers, such as Rodchenko and Man Ray). In this process, objects are

FIGURE 4
László Moholy-Nagy (1895–1946)
Untitled, 1936–46
photograph
9 x 13½ in. (22.9 x 34.3 cm), image size
Andrea Rosen Gallery

FIGURE 5
László Moholy-Nagy (1895–1946)
Untitled, 1940
photograph
13½ x 9 in. (34.3 x 22.9 cm), image size
Andrea Rosen Gallery

FIGURE 6
Margaret De Patta
Untitled photogram, 1939
gelatin silver print
7¼ x 9⅞ in (18.4 x 25.1 cm)
Ubu Gallery, New York &
Barry Friedman Limited, New York

FIGURE 7
Margaret De Patta
Untitled photogram, 1939
gelatin silver print
7 x 8⅝ in. (17.9 x 21.9 cm)
Ubu Gallery, New York &
Barry Friedman Limited, New York

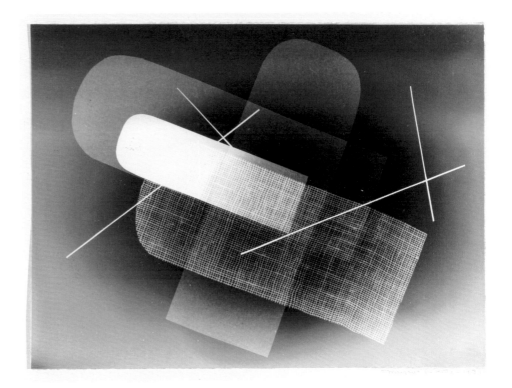

FIGURE 8
Alexander Rodchenko (1891–1956)
Composition, 1918
gouache and pencil on paper
13 x 6⅜ in. (33 x 16.2 cm)
Museum of Modern Art, New York, gift of the artist
Art © Estate of Alexander Rodchenko, RAO, Moscow;
VAGA, New York. Digital Image © The Museum of Modern
Art/Licensed by SCALA/Art Resource, NY

FIGURE 9
Margaret De Patta
Pin, c. 1947–50
sterling silver, coral, malachite
2¾ x 3⅜ x ⅜ in (69.9 x 85.7 x 9.5 mm)
Museum of Arts and Design, New York,
Gift of Eugene Bielawski, The Margaret De Patta Bequest,
through the American Craft Council, 1976

set directly on light-reactive paper, and a bulb is shone onto the assemblage, creating an image with "a wavering space between object and effect," in the words of historian Louis Kaplan.[7] In one of her photograms, De Patta scattered a handful of staples on the paper (fig. 7). Because one cannot tell which staples lie on top and which on the bottom, the photo stages an undetermined relationship of figure to ground. Such effects can be found elsewhere in Constructivism—not just in photos but in paintings and sculpture, too. Examples include El Lissitzky's use of translucency and overlapping in his Prouns, Rodchenko's tactile abstractions (fig. 8), or Moholy-Nagy's use of transparent Plexiglas. All of these experiments were formative for De Patta's jewelry, which often employed biomorphic cutouts of wire mesh or selective texturing of a surface in order to create a similar effect of dynamic layering (fig. 9).

De Patta was also powerfully influenced by Constructivist equilibrium studies: tabletop or ceiling-hung constructions in which disparate materials and formal elements were held in a tensely counterpoised asymmetry. Like Moholy-Nagy's sculptures, Alexander Calder's mobiles, or the plastic works of Naum Gabo (fig. 10), De Patta's own investigations of balance cleverly emphasized the principle of compositional autonomy (figs. 11, 12). Because each part of a Constructivist sculpture was offset (literally and figuratively) by one or more other parts, it could be viewed as self-regulating. All the relevant information was contained within the object itself.[8] It is easy to forget how radical the idea of a completely abstract sculpture was in the interwar period. Painting was one thing; even the least conventional canvas, bounded by its frame, is obviously a self-standing artwork. An abstract sculpture, on the other hand, is liable to come across as something else: ornament, furniture, or perhaps

an architectural model. This was a problem that all the early abstract sculptors faced, and they confronted it in varying ways. In Paris, Constantin Brancusi addressed it through his contrapuntal staging of bases, which built in a sort of aesthetic "buffer" between the work and the world.[9] The Italian Futurists, meanwhile, sought to invest their sculptures with a machine-like dynamism, not so much separated from the world as imposed upon it. In Umberto Boccioni's words, the objective was to "open up the figure like a window and enclose within it the environment in which it lives." The Futurist sculptural project was at once abstract and all-conquering: "Let us proclaim that the sidewalk can climb up your table, that your head can cross the street, and that at the same time your household lamp can suspend between one house and another the immense spiderweb of its dusty rays."[10]

The Constructivists shared this expansionist impulse—indeed, several of their number could claim direct affiliation with the Italians—but their understanding of the problem of sculpture was much more nuanced. Unlike the Futurists, they did not see artworks as direct means of transformation—as if they were weapons to be aimed at dusty museums and dull bourgeois. They were much closer in spirit to Theo Van Doesburg, Piet Mondrian, and the other members of the De Stijl movement in the Netherlands. Like the Dutch abstractionists, the Constructivists saw their sculptures as something like prototypes, created in a spirit of research: precursors of plastic forms that would eventually become universal. Their objects were radical, but also utopian. They aimed not only at the present but also at some better future. El Lissitzky memorably summarized this in his slogan, "I am not going to do this. You can do this." His Prouns were proposals, not assaults. The principle of equilibrium was key to this

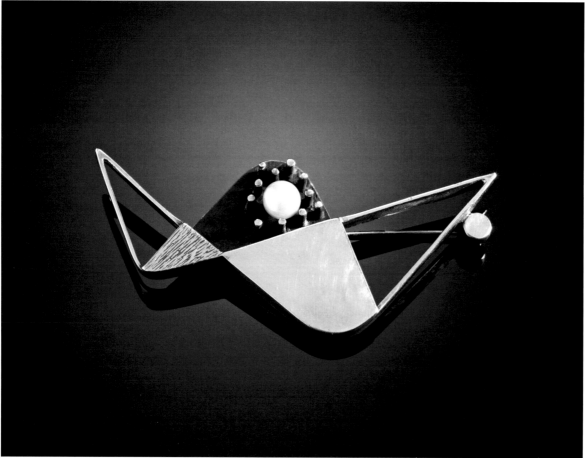

mode of operating, because it signaled a compositional strategy that could in theory be applied outside the work—but only by implication. A Constructivist sculpture was completely determined about its internal material relations. This means that the specific forms of the object could not be directly translated to another situation, but the relational structure itself—the structural principles of the work—could be applied elsewhere. Thus the notion of a perfectly balanced, but internally dynamic, artwork was a means of combining artistic purism with a radically expansive ideology.

How did De Patta incorporate these complex ideas into her jewelry? It cannot have been easy for her. The American studio crafts movement was a completely different context from that in which Constructivism had developed—much less politicized and theorized. Personally, too, she had none of the utopian instincts of the Russians. De Patta and her husband Eugene Bielawski were to the left politically—their names even appeared on a list of Communist sympathizers during the McCarthy era of "red hunting"—but while she certainly agreed with Tatlin's proclamation "the artist of material culture takes account of all properties of suitable materials and their interrelationships," it is hard to believe that she could have subscribed to his insistence that "we are now waging war for a collective way of life."[11] De Patta's perspective was that of a small-scale entrepreneur, individualist, and capitalist, not that of a proletarian "art worker." (In this respect, she is comparable to Edith Heath, who also was inspired by Moholy-Nagy's ideas about industrial experimentation and went on to found the West Coast's most stylish mass-production ceramics firm.[12])

On a more practical level, there were few Constructivist precedents for De Patta to follow in jewelry making per se. As a project in socialist aesthetics on the grandest scale, the movement had been opposed to luxury in any form, and its practitioners tended to treat ornament either as an incidental outcome or as a condition to be actively avoided. This was supposed to be style as politics, not as decoration. Yet the Constructivists also argued that their ideas could be applied to just about anything. They designed paintings and sculpture, buildings and graphics, clothing and crockery. Their hope was to reshape completely the everyday and to forge newly affective relations between people and the objects of their environment,[13] so a few of the Constructivists did dabble in jewelry alongside their many other activities. Rodchenko produced some enameled pins for the Russian state airline Dobrolet, for example, while Naum Slutzky and Anni Albers were among the Bauhaus artists who created jewelry along modernist lines, using metal and found objects (fig. 13). More important than the specifics of these minor forays, however, was the fact that Constructivism was a universal language of design. This meant that De Patta could use the movement's principles in her jewelry without any sense that she was misapplying them.

The most obvious thing that De Patta took from Constructivism was her approach to materials. She never selected a stone or a metal for its intrinsic value. This was of course a departure from traditional jewelry, in which the value of particular materials (diamonds, rubies, gold, silver) had always been of central importance. The notion that materials should be valued for their formal properties, not their preciousness, had wide currency

FIGURE 10
Naum Gabo (1890–1977)
Construction in Space with Balance on Two Points,
c. 1925–26
cellulose acetate, polymethyl methacrylate (Plexiglas)
10⅝ x 13¾ x 6½ in. (27.1 x 34.9 x 16.5 cm), with base
Harvard Art Museums, Busch-Reisinger Museum,
Gift of Lydia Dorner in memory of Dr. Alexander Dorner

FIGURE 11
Margaret De Patta
Sketch for production pin #9, 1947
graphite on paper
3 x 5 in. (7.6 x 12.7 cm)
Margaret De Patta Archives, Bielawski
Trust, Point Richmond, California

FIGURE 12
Margaret De Patta
Production Pin #9,
designed 1947, produced 1947–57
sterling silver, pearl
1½ x 3¼ x ⅜ in. (38 x 83 x 10 mm)
Collection of the Oakland Museum of California,
Gift of Sylvia and Eric Elsesser

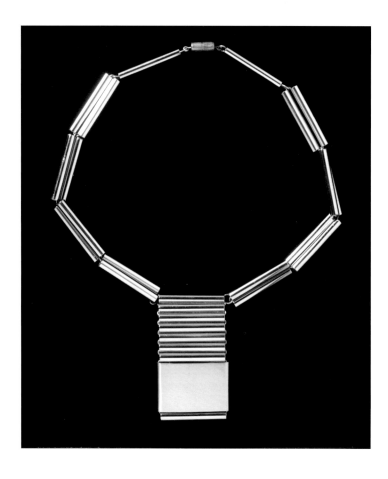

FIGURE 13
Naum Slutzky (1894–1965)
Necklace, 1930
chromium-plated brass
2⅝ x 1½ in (67 x 38 mm), pendant;
10 in. (254 mm), chain (in two parts);
additional shorter fine chain
Victoria and Albert Museum, London

among interwar jewelers, who were tired of making luxurious *bijouterie*. The French art deco designer Gérard Sandoz, for example, said: "Let us have no preconceptions as to materials. Personally, I consider that before everything else, one must think of the line and the general volume of the piece of jewelry to be created."[14] De Patta was in full agreement with this sentiment, but she also applied a specifically Constructivist logic to her materials. For her, a stone or metal was important only if it dictated particular formal solutions. Rather than inventing a form and then selecting materials to suit, she chose her materials and then crafted a design around and through them. This can be seen in the way she twisted pliant silver wire to create volumetric, linear designs (reminiscent, again, of Moholy-Nagy's photographs) or in her use of multiple pebbles as ovoid counterweights. She did use semiprecious stones, but only because of their formal properties: rutilated quartz for its floating linear inclusions; black pearls for their ability to punctuate a field of reflective silver; faceted quartz crystals for the way they visually multiplied linear elements placed behind them. For her, even the transparency of a stone could be a formal principle, analogous to the use of glass in modernist architecture or plastic in Constructivist sculpture (figs. 14, 15).[15]

De Patta also embraced the Constructivist challenge of achieving dynamism within a balanced composition. As a jeweler, she developed this idea by considering the way in which the active equilibrium would "perform" when pinned or draped on a moving body. While she was at pains to emphasize the autonomy of her jewels, calling them "wearable sculptures" and having them photographed against neutral backdrops rather than on models, she also took an active interest in the body's geometry.

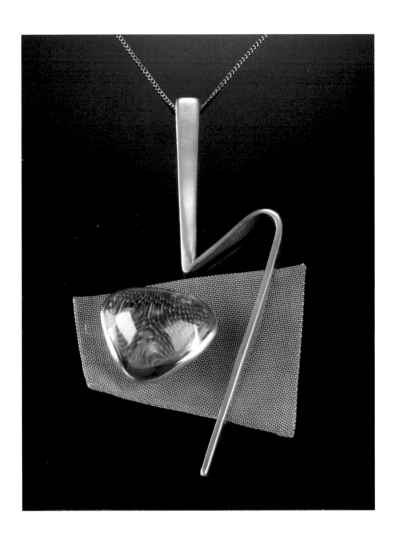

FIGURE 14
Margaret De Patta
Pendant, 1950
sterling silver, stainless steel screen, quartz
4 x 3 x 1¼ in. (102 x 76 x 32 mm), without chain
Collection of the Oakland Museum of California,
Gift of Eugene Bielawski, The Margaret
De Patta Memorial Collection

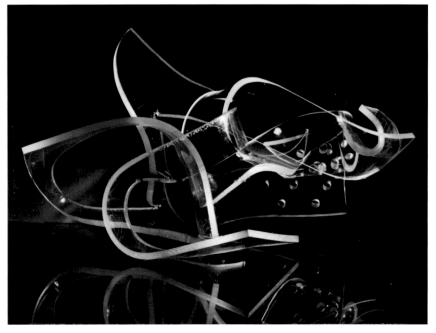

FIGURE 15
László Moholy-Nagy (1895–1946)
Plexiglas sculpture, 1946
gelatin silver print
7¼ x 9¾ in. (18.4 x 24.6 cm)
Courtesy of George Eastman House,
International Museum of Photography and Film

This is most obvious in her rings, which engage the fingers inventively with encircling elements or perch asymmetrically across multiple fingers. But even her preferred forms—pendants and brooches, which stand apart from the body even as they ornament it—take some of their drama from the way they stay balanced even as they move through space. While her use of extreme cantilevered forms shows a clear debt to Lissitzky's asymmetrical Prouns (figs. 16, 17), they are arguably distinctive in that they inhabit real, rather than pictorial, space.

De Patta also proved ingenious in her application of the Constructivist principle of functionalism in which every element within a work serves a direct purpose. Here she perhaps did have a strong sense of precedent, because function is no more obviously relevant within an abstract sculpture than in a piece of jewelry. In each case, the answer was to treat structure as its own self-legitimating arena of action. Each part of the object (whether sculpture or jewel) serves a double purpose, establishing a form and holding it together at the same time. In this respect the Constructivist object could be compared to a work of engineering, such as a bridge or an airplane; though such things are certainly inventive, and may be formally beautiful, all their parts are conceived as integrated and necessary, rather than independent or arbitrary. There is an element of pretense in applying this same logic to a nonfunctional object, of course, but it was nonetheless a leap of imagination that led to extraordinarily rigorous design solutions.

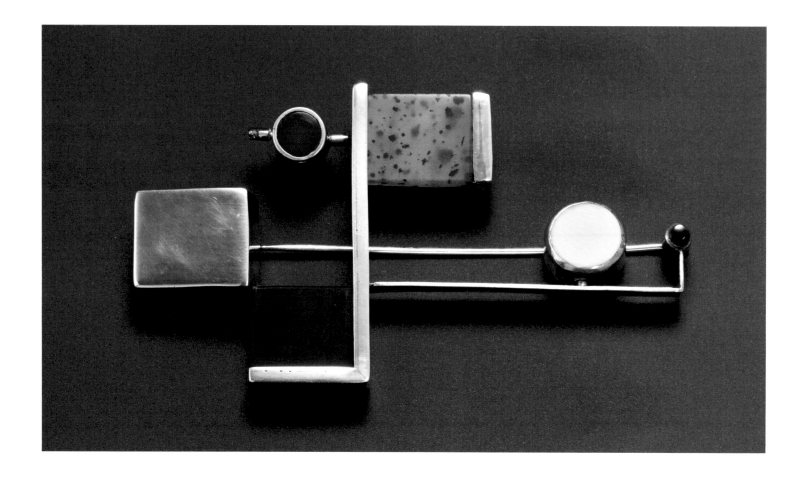

The results can be seen in a De Patta pin of 1950 in which semi-precious stones and white gold are set into a Mondrian-like grid that is partly implied and partly "drawn" in linear silver bars and wire (fig. 18). The strongest graphic element is the backwards *L* at the center of the composition, which is also the structural core of the piece. It is the primary constructive element, equally important in form and function. Behind the *L* runs a thin wire, squared at the right end to create two parallel lines. The back of the wire can be pinned into the wearer's clothing, but also marks the midpoint of the counter-balanced square and circle that act as the composition's lateral anchors. The front of the wire, similarly, is continued visually

FIGURE 18

Margaret De Patta

Pin, 1950

sterling silver, white gold, amber, coral, malachite, onyx, moss agate

1½ x 3 x ¼ in. (38 x 76 x 6 mm)

Collection of the Oakland Museum of California, Gift of Eugene Bielawski, The Margaret De Patta Memorial Collection

by the top and bottom edges of the two squares to the left. At the top of the pin, the white gold bar that marks the edge of a square (a thin plaque of moss agate) both acts as its functional setting, holding it in tension, and also is the midpoint between the L and the white circle to the right. Finally, a small concentric circle at upper left punctuates the composition. (Like the white circle at the lower right, it is a kinetic element that can be spun around to change the color balance of the design.) It echoes the larger circular element to the right, and it also helps to define the rectangle contained within the L as three equal square zones, stacked vertically: black square, negative space, concentric circle.

It is worth inspecting all of De Patta's works in this way, looking for these finely calibrated relations, because that is exactly how she was thinking when she made them. There is, throughout her jewelry, a combination of intricacy and structural integrity. This was the most important thing she drew from Constructivism: its density of internal reference. And this leads us to the question of De Patta's relevance within the broader history of jewelry. Craft is typically viewed as defined by its supplementarity.[16] Unlike the fine art disciplines, it is fundamentally relational. This has both positive and negative aspects. On the one hand, craft is seen as integrated with everyday experience, and therefore humane and life affirming. On the other, it is considered to be quite literally of secondary importance in comparison to fine art—forever installed in the backseat. This is a structural matter; it's not so much that craft activities are intrinsically inferior, but rather that supplemental forms and activities will inevitably be labeled as craft. So, put in simple terms, there is no getting out of the bind of supplementarity.

De Patta's approach to form, however, cannot be captured within a simple binary of art vs. craft. Like the Constructivists before her, she saw that it was possible to nest autonomous form within a manifestly supplemental genre. (The design prototype arguably functioned for Lissitzky and Moholy-Nagy just as the brooch or pendant did for De Patta—in both cases, pure abstraction was caught within a larger "applied" structure). So what can we learn from her today? She was, after all, a high modernist. Her best works were made half a century ago, and the ideas she explored had been developed three decades earlier still, in Russia and Germany. Yet her conviction that every element of a piece of jewelry should bear its own weight, even as it relates to everything around it, has an ethical implication that is still relevant. For all their abstraction, the Constructivists were all trying to model an egalitarian society, its freedom limited only by a demand for rich correspondences. De Patta believed in this, too, but the difference is that she was able to conceive this project in non-totalized terms. For the Constructivists it was all or nothing: constant struggle, until the world could be reborn. Everything De Patta did was infused with a sense of purpose, but she was no radical. She felt no need to insist that everything should remake itself in the image of her work. For her, a compartmentalized perfection was enough. Today, this more pragmatic and less imposing view seems increasingly attractive. Perhaps it's not what De Patta learned from Constructivism that is most inspiring, but what she felt she could leave behind.

1

Margaret De Patta and Eugene Bielawski, book manuscript, undated and unpaginated; Margaret De Patta Archives, Bielawski Trust, Point Richmond, California.

2

El Lissitzky et al., "The First Working Group of Constructivists, " 1924, translated in John Bowlt, *Russian Art of the Avant Garde: Theory and Criticism 1902–1934* (London: Thames and Hudson, 1988), 241.

3

For examples see Lázsló Moholy-Nagy, *The New Vision* (Minneola, N. Y.: Dover Publications, 2005; org. pub., 1938).

4

Lázsló Moholy-Nagy, Raoul Hausmann, Hans Arp, and Ivan Puni, "Manifesto of Elemental Art," 1921, quoted in Rainer K. Wick, *Teaching at the Bauhaus* (Ostfildern-Ruit: Hatje Cantz, 2000), 124.

5

Margaret De Patta, notes and sketches, ca. 1940–41, Margaret De Patta Archive, Oakland Museum of California.

6

Yoshiko Uchida, "Jewelry by Margaret De Patta," *Craft Horizons* 25, no. 2 (March–April, 1965): 23.

7

Louis Kaplan, *Lázsló Moholy-Nagy: Biographical Writings* (Durham: Duke University Press, 1995), 90.

8

This idea was of great importance to the postwar American theorists of Constructivism, the art historian Rosalind Krauss and her sometime partner Robert Morris. Both saw the complex autonomy of Constructivist sculptures as a model for art that was internally dynamic but still separate (and hence potentially critical). See Rosalind Krauss, *Passages in Modern Sculpture* (Cambridge: MIT Press, 1977); Robert Morris, *Continuous Project Altered Daily* (Cambridge: MIT Press, 1993).

9

Anna C. Chave, *Constantin Brancusi: Shifting the Bases of Art* (New Haven: Yale University Press, 1993).

10

Umberto Boccioni, "Technical Manifesto of Futurist Sculpture," 1912, http://www.unknown.nu/futurism/techsculpt.html (accessed 20 September 2010).

11

Vladimir Tatlin, "The Problem of the Relationship between Man and Object," 1930, translated and reprinted in Larisa Zhadova, *Tatlin* (London: Thames and Hudson, 1988).

12

Amos Klausner, *Heath Ceramics: The Complexity of Simplicity* (San Francisco: Chronicle Books, 2006), 22–23.

13

Christina Kaier, *Imagine No Possessions: The Socialist Objects of Russian Constructivism* (Cambridge: MIT Press, 2005).

14

Quoted in S. Raulet, *Art Deco Jewellery* (London: Thames and Hudson, 2002), 173. I am indebted to Roberta Bernabei for this reference.

15

Margaret De Patta, "From the Inside," *The Palette* 32, no. 2 (spring 1952): 15.

16

Glenn Adamson, *Thinking Through Craft* (Oxford: Berg Publishers, 2007).

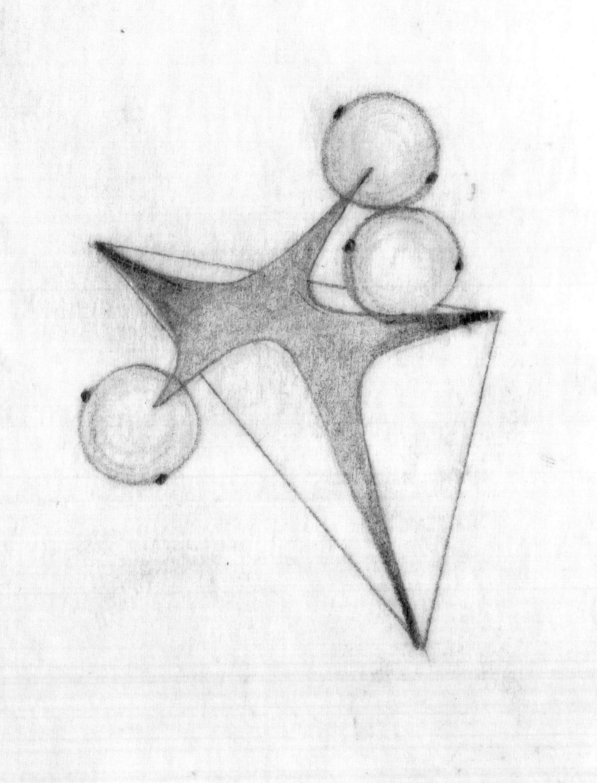

Mrs Johnson — Pin - Ring

4 Amethysts mounted
in silver and white gold

Pin ———— 100.00
Ring ———— 60.00

Tax not included

Pin — 14 K white gold or
yellow gold — 145.00

Ring — 14 K gold — 100.00

PLATE 1
Margaret De Patta
Pendant, 1959
white gold, ebony, faceted quartz
3¾ x 1 x 2½ in. (95 x 25 x 64 mm)
Collection of the Oakland Museum of California,
Gift of Eugene Bielawski, The Margaret De Patta Memorial Collection

PLATE 2
Margaret De Patta
Pin, 1956
sterling silver, quartz, epoxy enamel paint
1 ⅞ x 3 ¾ x ½ in. (48 x 95 x 13 mm)
Collection of the Oakland Museum of California,
Gift of Eugene Bielawski, The Margaret De Patta Memorial Collection

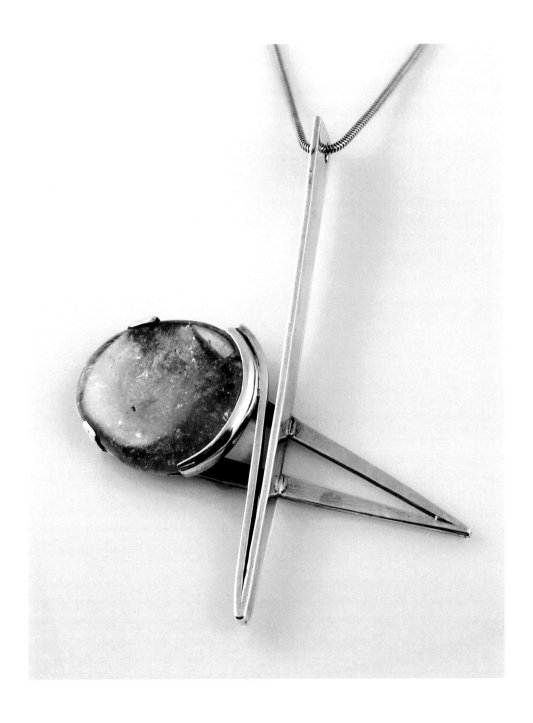

Margaret De Patta
Pendant, 1954
white gold, green tourmaline
4 x 3¼ x ¼ in. (102 x 83 x 6 mm)
Collection of Leslie Simons

PLATE 4
Margaret De Patta
Neckpiece, c. 1955
sterling silver, quartz
6 x 4½ x 1⅛ in. (152 x 114 x 29 mm)
Collection of Leslie Simons

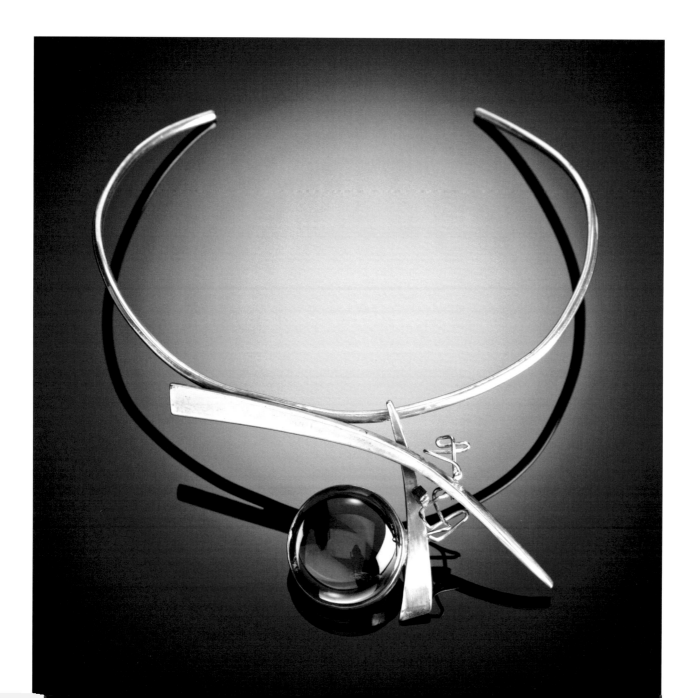

PLATE 5
Margaret De Patta
Pendant, c. 1953
gold, smoky quartz, pearl
2¹⁄₈ x 1⁷⁄₈ x 1⁵⁄₈
(54 x 48 x 41 mm), without chain
Margaret De Patta Archives,
Bielawski Trust, Point Richmond,
California

PLATE 6

Margaret De Patta

Ring, 1941

gold, quartz, cultured pearl

1¼ x ¾ x ⅞ in. (32 x 19 x 22 mm)

Collection of the Oakland Museum of California,

Gift of Eugene Bielawski, The Margaret De Patta Memorial Collection

PLATE 7

Margaret De Patta

Ring, 1947

quartz, white gold, black onyx

1⅛ x ¾ x ⅞ in. (29 x 19 x 22 mm)

Collection of the Oakland Museum of California,

Gift of Eugene Bielawski, The Margaret De Patta Memorial Collection

PLATE 8
Margaret De Patta
Ring, c. 1944–45
gold, onyx, coral
1⅛ x ⅞ x 1⅛ in. (29 x 22 x 29 mm)
Collection of Leslie Simons

PLATE 9
Margaret De Patta
Ring, c. 1948
sterling silver, quartz, hematite
⅝ x ⅞ x 1¼ in. (16 x 22 x 31 mm)
Montreal Museum of Fine Arts,
Liliane and David M. Stewart Collection, Gift of Paul Leblanc

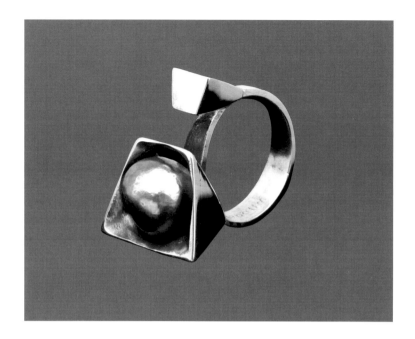

PLATE 10
Margaret De Patta
Ring, 1953
white gold, baroque pearl
⅞ x ⅝ x 1⅛ in. (23 x 19 x 29 mm)
Smithsonian American Art Museum,
Museum purchase

PLATE 11
Margaret De Patta
Earrings, 1944
sterling silver, moonstone
½ x ⅞ x ¾ in. (13 x 22 x 19 mm)
Collection of Steven Cabella

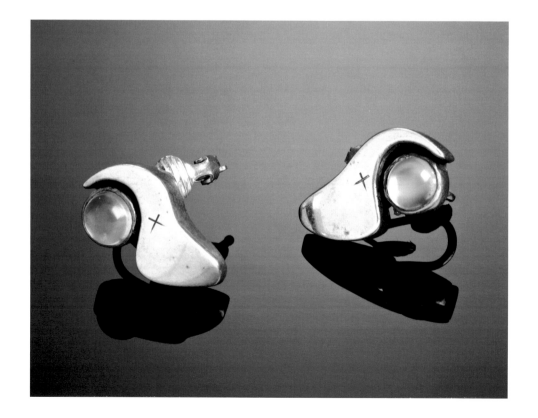

PLATE 12
Margaret De Patta
Cuff bracelet, c. 1955
gold, smoky topaz
2³⁄₈ x 2¹⁄₂ x 1⁷⁄₈ in. (60 x 64 x 48 mm)
Collection of Toby Bielawski

PLATE 13
Margaret De Patta
Earrings, c. 1949
sterling silver
2 1/8 x 5/8 x 7/8 in.
(56 x 16 x 24 mm)
Montreal Museum of Fine Arts,
Liliane and David M. Stewart
Collection, Gift of Paul Leblanc

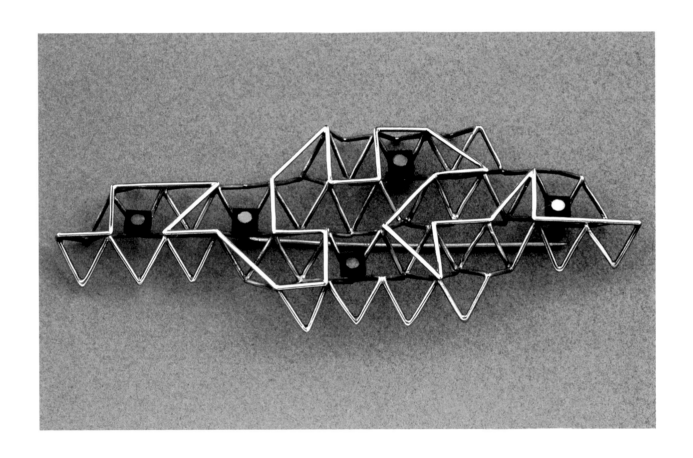

PLATE 14
Margaret De Patta
Pin, c. 1957
gold, onyx, jade, coral
1³/₄ x 4⁵/₈ x ¹/₂ in. (44 x 117 x 13 mm)
Private collection

PLATE 15
Margaret De Patta
Earrings, c. 1955
sterling silver, white gold, rutilated quartz
2⅝ x ⅞ x ¾ in. (67 x 24 x 20 mm)
Montreal Museum of Fine Arts,
Liliane and David M. Stewart Collection, Gift of Paul Leblanc

PLATE 16
Margaret De Patta
Pin, 1946
sterling silver
2½ x 3½ x ¼ in.
(64 x 89 x 6 mm)
Museum of Fine Arts, Boston,
The Daphne Farago Collection

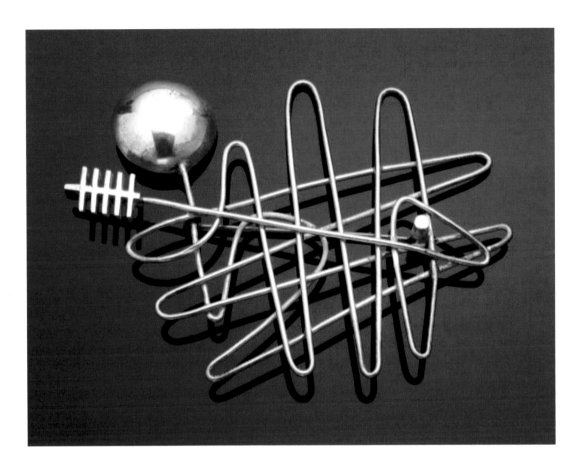

PLATE 17
Margaret De Patta
Ring, 1949
white gold, rutilated quartz
⅞ x ¾ x 1 in. (22 x 19 x 25 mm)
Margaret De Patta Archives, Bielawski Trust,
Point Richmond, California

PLATE 18
Margaret De Patta
Pin, c. 1953
sterling silver, agate
3¾ x 2⅜ x ⅞ in. (95 x 60 x 22 mm)
Collection of Metal Arts Guild, San Francisco

PLATE 19
Margaret De Patta
Pin, c. 1950
sterling silver, quartz, glass bead
3 x 1¾ x 1¾ in. (76 x 44 x 44 mm)
Collection of Hattula Moholy-Nagy

PLATE 20
Margaret De Patta
Ring, 1954
white gold, rutilated quartz, black onyx
1 x ⅞ x ¾ in. (25 x 22 x 19 mm)
Museum of Arts and Design, New York,
Gift of Eugene Bielawski, The Margaret De Patta Bequest,
through the American Craft Council, 1976

PLATE 21
Margaret De Patta
Pin, 1942
sterling silver, black onyx, quartz
2 x 1¾ in. (51 x 45 mm)
Collection of the Oakland Museum of California,
bequest of David Hyman

PLATE 23
Margaret De Patta
Pin, c. 1959
sterling silver, beach pebbles, pearl
2³⁄₈ x 2½ x ½ in. (60 x 64 x 13 mm)
Montreal Museum of Fine Arts,
Liliane and David M. Stewart Collection, Gift of Paul Leblanc

PLATE 24
Margaret De Patta
Pin, c. 1957
sterling silver, beach pebbles, pearl
2 x 3½ x ⅝ in. (51 x 89 x 16 mm)
Collection of Forrest L. Merrill

PLATE 25
Margaret De Patta
Watch bracelet, c.1962
sterling silver, onyx
2 ½ x 2⅛ x 1 in. (64 x 54 x 25 mm)
Collection of the Oakland Museum of California,
Art Deaccession Fund

PLATE 26
Margaret De Patta
Pin, 1941
sterling silver, moss agate, onyx
1 x 1¼ x ¼ in. (25 x 32 x 6 mm)
Collection of the Oakland Museum of California,
Gift of Eugene Bielawski, The Margaret
De Patta Memorial Collection

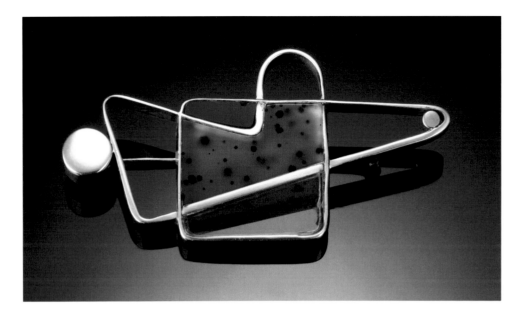

PLATE 28 [BELOW]
Margaret De Patta
Pin, 1943
sterling silver, onyx
1¾ x 2¼ x ½ in. (45 x 57 x 13 mm)
Private collection

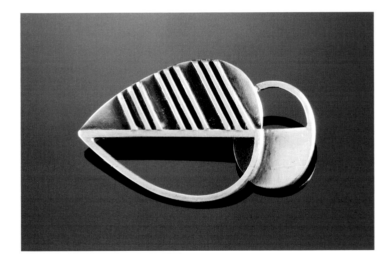

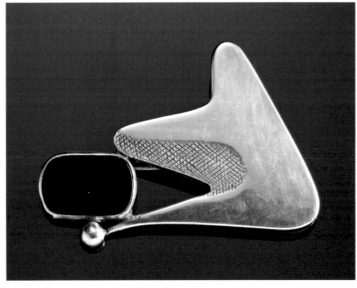

PLATE 27 [ABOVE]
Margaret De Patta
Pin, 1941
sterling silver
1 x 1¼ x ¼ in. (25 x 45 x 6 mm)
Collection of Steven Cabella

PLATE 29
Margaret De Patta
Pin, 1960
gold, topaz, peridot
3 x 2½ x ⅞ in. (76 x 64 x 22 mm)
Collection of the Oakland Museum of California,
Gift of Eugene Bielawski, The Margaret
De Patta Memorial Collection

PLATE 30
Margaret De Patta
Pendant, 1961
14k gold, ebony
9½ x 4¾ x ¾ in. (241 x 121 x 19 mm)
Museum of Arts and Design, New York,
Gift of Eugene Bielawski, The Margaret De Patta Bequest,
through the American Craft Council, 1976

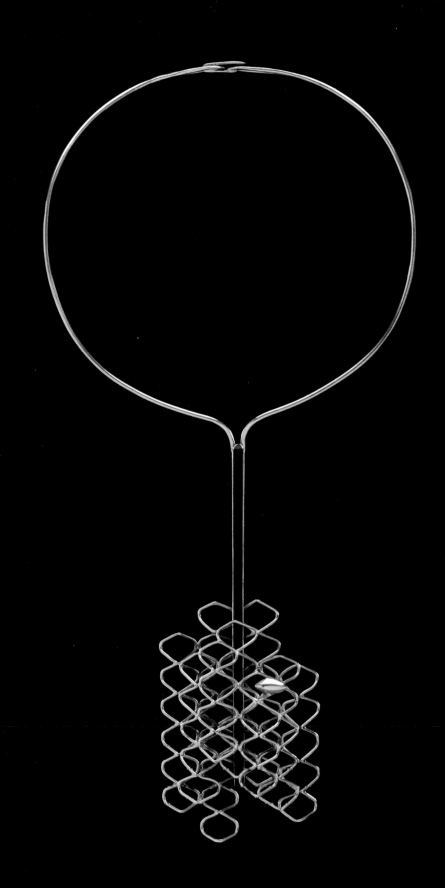

PLATE 31
Margaret De Patta
Ring, c.1933
sterling silver, black enamel
2 x 1½ x ½ in. (51 x 38 x 13 mm)
Collection of the Oakland Museum of California,
Gift of Eugene Bielawski, The Margaret
De Patta Memorial Collection

PLATE 32
Margaret De Patta
Bracelet, c. 1933
sterling silver
1¼ x 2⅛ in. (32 x 54 mm)
Collection of the Oakland Museum of California,
Gift of Eugene Bielawski, The Margaret
De Patta Memorial Collection

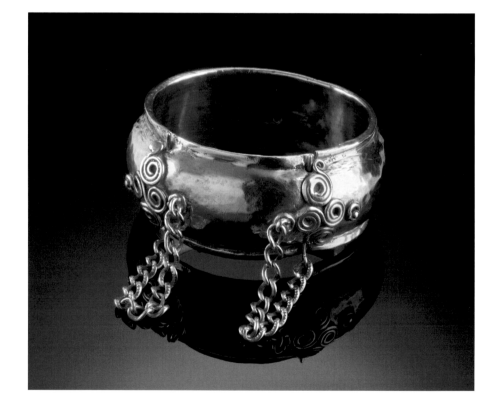

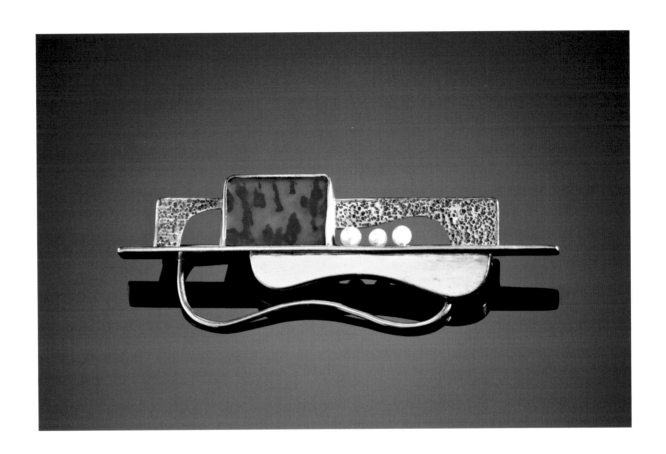

PLATE 33
Margaret De Patta
Pin, c. 1939
14k gold, pearls, moss agate
⅞ x 2⅝ x ¼ in. (22 x 67 x 6 mm)
Private collection

PLATE 34
Margaret De Patta
Salad servers, 1937; *baby spoon*, 1944; *fork*, c. 1935
sterling silver, copper
salad servers: 8⅛ x ⅝ x 2 in. (20.6 x 1.6 x 5.8 cm), each
baby spoon: 3 x 1 x 1¼ in. (7.6 x 2.5 x 3.2 cm)
fork: 6½ x ¾ x 1 in. (16.5 x 1.9 x 2.5 cm)
Private collection

PLATE 35
Margaret De Patta
Flatware, c. 1936–37
sterling silver, copper, stainless steel
salad fork: 6⅜ x 1 x ½ in. (16.2 x 2.5 x 1.3 cm)
dinner fork: 7¼ x 1 x ½ in. (18.4 x 2.5 x 1.3 cm)
knife: 9¼ x ⅞ x ⅝ in. (23.5 x 2.2 x 1.6 cm)
spoon: 6⅛ x 1⅜ x ½ in. (15.6 x 3.5 x 1.3 cm)
Dallas Museum of Art, The Patsy Lacy Griffith Collection,
Gift of Patsy Lacy Griffith by exchange

Rutilated Crystal

cut ③

3

14½

13

9½

"...a creative social

Rutiles crosswise

artist has a responsibility..."

m

dius = inside curve of rwq

Size No 11

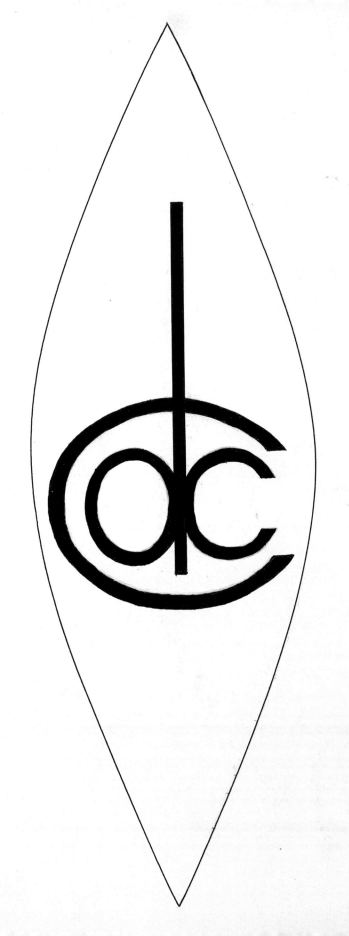

Jewelry for a Never-Increasing Minority

Margaret De Patta in the Marketplace

JULIE M. MUÑIZ

"It seems to me that a creative artist has a social responsibility [to] produce not the single highly-priced handmade article for extremely limited consumption but to produce the best possible in design, workmanship, and materials and give pleasure to the largest number of people possible."[1]

A socialist and supporter of the postwar labor movement, Margaret De Patta held strong convictions about her social responsibility as a jewelry artist. Art should be for everyone, she felt, not just for the wealthy. Attempting to make good design more affordable to a larger public, in 1946 she boldly attempted what some of her colleagues thought unthinkable: limited serial production of her jewelry designs.[2] Looking back on her decision in an essay for *Arts & Architecture* the following year, she wrote: "Here then was the aim—to produce more than one piece of each design and to sell these pieces at a lower cost. . . . I wanted to place my designs upon the market at a figure to compete with the comparable material quality costume jewelry."[3]

Many signs indicated that the time was right for such an endeavor. Yet Designs Contemporary,[4] the business Margaret De Patta and her husband, Eugene Bielawski, founded to market limited production jewelry to "an ever-increasing minority"[5] (figs. 1,2), was never a financial success, and the couple was forced to stop production after only eleven years in business.

FIGURE 1
Margaret De Patta
Working drawing of Designs Contemporary logo, c. 1947–57
ink and graphite on card stock
14½ x 10½ in. (36.8 x 26.7 cm)
Margaret De Patta Archives, Bielawski Trust, Point Richmond, California

FIGURE 2
Jewelry by Margaret De Patta announcement card, c. 1947
ink on card stock
3 x 5½ in. (7.6 x 14 cm)
Margaret De Patta Archives, Bielawski Trust, Point Richmond, California

The failure of the production line highlights the inherent conflict between De Patta's Bauhaus-inspired social, political, and economic ideals and her need to express herself artistically through concepts, materials, and techniques suited to one-of-a-kind studio production. Moreover, despite De Patta's desire and efforts to educate Americans, most were not able to appreciate her innovative designs.

Prior to her attempt at limited production, De Patta had already established a name for herself in modernist and jewelry circles. She had been selling her studio jewelry through the San Francisco craft gallery Amberg-Hirth for over a decade. More significantly, she had participated in a series of exhibitions that brought her talents to the attention of ever more influential audiences, culminating in her inclusion in the Museum of Modern Art's 1946 exhibition *Modern Handmade Jewelry.*

De Patta also drew attention to herself because of her political associations. Between 1944 and 1947, she taught at and served as chairman of the Basic Design Workshop at the Tom Mooney Labor School in San Francisco (later called the California Labor School). Eugene Bielawski, whom she met when she attended the School of Design in Chicago in 1940 and 1941, became director of arts at the institution in 1945. In addition to art and design classes, the Labor School offered courses such as "What Is Coalition?" "Soviet Union, 1917–47," and "Economic Theories of Marx and Keynes." The school's strong political bent led to a three-year investigation from 1947 through 1949 by the California Senate Fact-Finding Committee on Un-American Activities, with the Committee concluding that the school was one of California's "Red centers of intrigue and treachery. . .under the complete control and domination of the Communist Party."[6] In 1948, the U.S. Attorney General placed the institution on the List of Subversive Organizations. As a result of their association with the school,

De Patta and Bielawski were blacklisted by the Joint Fact-Finding Committee of the California Legislature for three years, from 1947 through 1949.

De Patta was a self-employed artisan, so the legislature's censure meant little to her bottom line. For Bielawski, however, the consequences were dire. After refusing to sign a loyalty oath, Bielawski could no longer find work as a teacher. This is likely a factor in his increased involvement in De Patta's jewelry business.

According to many of their friends, it was Bielawski who conceived of the production line, swaying De Patta with their shared belief in "design for all." Philosophically, De Patta supported the line. In actuality, she was ambivalent about production and its boring repetitive process, even disapproving of the use of casting, which she felt "destroys the characteristics of the metal."[7] She kept these feelings mostly to herself, however, and together she and Bielawski arrived at a solution that worked for both of them: De Patta designed and crafted each of the original designs, and Bielawski applied his technical expertise to developing and refining the casting process (fig. 3). In addition, Bielawski took on the tedious task of casting and finishing each piece himself, with occasional help from a hired assistant.[8]

The original 1946 line included only eight pieces: four rings, three brooches, and one set of earrings or cufflinks.[9] The following year, the line increased to thirty-one pieces, including nineteen rings (fig. 4), and by 1949 the total reached forty-one (fig. 6). In 1953, the popularity of wedding bands prompted new designs and a promotion, bringing the total number of production pieces to sixty-one (fig. 5).[10] By 1955, De Patta had designs sketched and ready for one hundred six pieces, although it appears that no more than the first sixty-one were serially

FIGURE 3
Designs Contemporary
Molds for production pieces #22, #9, and #6, c. 1947
rubber
TOP: 1 x 3 x 1 in. (18.2 x 7.0 x 2.5 cm),
CENTER: 4 x 3 x 1 in. (10.2 x 7.6 x 2.5 cm),
BOTTOM: 4¼ x 3¾ x 1 in. (10.8 x 9.5 x 2.5 cm)
Margaret De Patta Archives, Bielawski Trust,
Point Richmond, California

FIGURE 4
Margaret De Patta
Production rings as photographed by artist, c. 1947
BACK, LEFT TO RIGHT: *#20, #7, #2, #1, #3;*
CENTER: *#1, #29, #18, #17;*
FRONT: *#19, #16*
Margaret De Patta Archives, Bielawski Trust,
Point Richmond, California

111

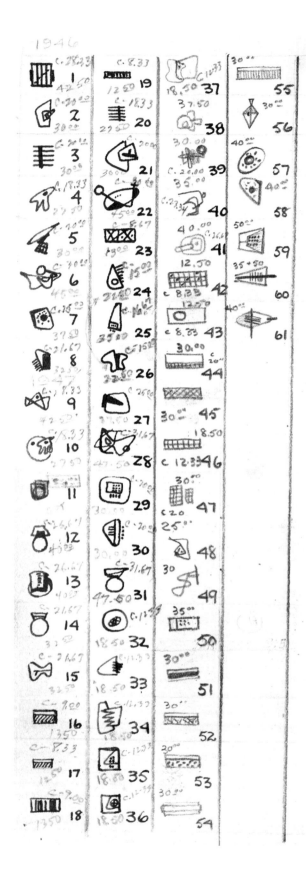

produced. Ranging in price from thirteen to fifty dollars, the complete line was comprised of thirty-three rings (seventeen were wedding bands), fifteen brooches, and thirteen pairs of earrings/cufflinks.

From the start, De Patta and Bielawski were organized in their undertaking, giving each design a production number to allow for easy identification and ordering[11] and developing a written statement that detailed their policy concerning minimum purchase requirements for retailers in exchange for an "exclusive territory franchise."[12] De Patta and Bielawski modified the policy in the first two years of production to require a minimum wholesale purchase of two hundred dollars in order to carry the line.[13] Only after the initial investment were retailers allowed to take jewelry on consignment—a savvy business decision that not only ensured orders upfront but also provided stronger motivation for retailers to sell their inventory.

Through their combined efforts, the couple succeeded in attracting retailers in major cities across the country.[14] The majority of shops taking on the Designs Contemporary production line, such as Van Keppel–Green in Beverly Hills and Cargoes in San Francisco, retailed modern designs in furnishings and housewares alongside her jewelry; a few, such as Nanny's in San Francisco, specialized in jewelry or other small handicrafts. Many outlets sold De Patta's one-of-a-kind creations, or Originals, as she called them, as well as her production line, and many also brokered special commissions.[15]

FIGURE 5 [LEFT]
Margaret De Patta
*"Original De Patta Productions" from
De Patta design book,* c. 1946–53
Collection of the Oakland Museum
of California, Gift of Eugene Bielawski,
The Margaret De Patta Memorial
Collection

FIGURE 6 [RIGHT]
Margaret De Patta
*Production jewelry as photographed
by the artist,* 1949
Margaret De Patta Archives,
Bielawski Trust, Point Richmond,
California

FIRST ROW (LEFT TO RIGHT)

Production ring #1
designed 1942, produced 1946–57
sterling silver with clear or smoky
crystal, $42.50 retail

Production ring #2
designed 1943, produced 1946–57
sterling silver, $30.00 retail

**Production ring #3 (man's ring)
and #20 (woman's ring)**
designed 1944, produced 1946–57
sterling silver, $27.50–$30.00 retail

Production pin #4
designed 1944, produced 1946–57
sterling silver, $27.50 retail

Production pin #5
designed 1944, produced 1946–57
sterling silver, $30.00 retail

Production pin #6
designed 1946, produced 1946–57
sterling silver with clear crystal,
$45.00 retail

Production ring #7
designed 1946, produced 1946–57
sterling silver with cultured pearl,
$37.50 retail

Production ring #8
designed 1946, produced 1946–57
sterling silver with black onyx or jade,
$32.50 retail

Production pin #9
designed 1947, produced 1947–57
sterling silver with cultured pearl,
$37.50 retail

SECOND ROW (LEFT TO RIGHT)

Production pin #10
designed 1943, produced 1947–57
sterling silver, $27.50 retail

Production ring #11
(not pictured)
discontinued in 1947

Production ring #12
designed 1941, produced 1947–57
sterling silver with clear, flat top
crystal, $40.00 retail

Production ring #13
designed 1947, produced 1947–57
sterling silver with black onyx,
$40.00 retail

Production ring #14
designed 1947, produced 1947–48
sterling silver with hawk's eye, red
jasper, or Wyoming jade, $32.50 retail

Production pin #15,
(see fig. 10)
designed 1947, produced 1947–48
sterling silver, $32.50 retail

**Production ring #16 (man's ring)
and #17 (woman's ring)**
designed 1947, produced 1947–57
sterling silver, $12.50–$13.50 retail
14K gold, $37.50–$45.00 retail

**Production ring #18 (man's size)
and #19 (woman's size)**
designed 1947, produced 1947–57
sterling silver, $12.50–$13.50 retail
14K gold, $35.00–$40.00 retail

Production ring #21
designed 1947, produced 1947–57
sterling silver, $30.00 retail

Production pin #22
designed 1947, produced 1947–57
sterling silver with clear crystal,
$45.00 retail

Production ring #23
designed 1947, produced 1947–57
sterling silver, $13.00 retail
14K gold, $50.00 retail

THIRD ROW (LEFT TO RIGHT)

**Production earrings or
cufflinks #24**
designed 1943, produced 1947–57
sterling silver, $30.00 retail

**Production earrings or
cufflinks #25**
designed 1943, produced 1947–57
sterling silver, $25.00 retail

**Production earrings or
cufflinks #26**
designed 1942, produced 1947–57
sterling silver, $30.00 retail

Production ring #27
designed 1947, produced 1947–57
black onyx, red jasper, or
Wyoming jade
sterling silver, $37.50 retail
14K gold, $75.00 retail

Production pin #28
(not pictured)
designed 1947, produced 1947–57
sterling silver with semi-precious
stones, $47.50 retail

Production ring #29
designed 1942, produced 1947–57
sterling silver, $30.00 retail

Production ring #30
designed 1947, produced 1947–57
sterling silver, $30.00 retail

Production ring #31
designed 1947, produced 1947–57
sterling silver with rutilated crystal,
$47.50 retail

**Production earrings or
cufflinks #32**
designed 1948, produced 1948–57
sterling silver, $18.50 retail

**Production earrings or
cufflinks #33**
designed 1944, produced 1948–57
sterling silver, $18.50 retail

FOURTH ROW (LEFT TO RIGHT)

**Production earrings or
cufflinks #34**
designed 1943, produced 1948–57
sterling silver, $18.50 retail

**Production earrings or
cufflinks #35**
designed 1948, produced 1948–57
sterling silver, $18.50 retail

**Production earrings or
cufflinks #36**
designed 1941, produced 1948–57
sterling silver, $18.50 retail

**Production earrings or
cufflinks #37**
designed 1948, produced 1948–57
sterling silver, $18.50 retail

Production pin #38
designed 1949, produced 1949–57
sterling silver, $37.50 retail

Production pin #39
designed 1946, produced 1949–57
sterling silver, $30.00 retail

Production pin #40
designed 1949, produced 1949–57
sterling silver, $35.00 retail

Production pin #41
designed 1949, produced 1949–57
sterling silver with stainless steel
screen, $40.00 retail

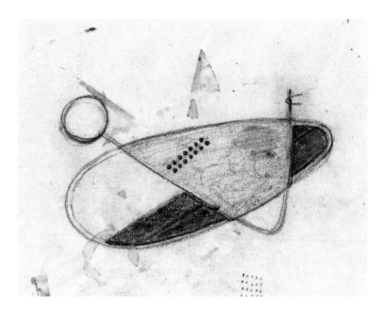

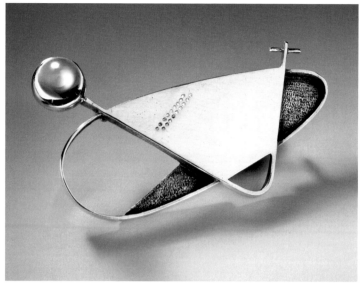

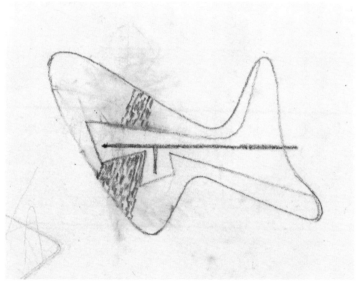

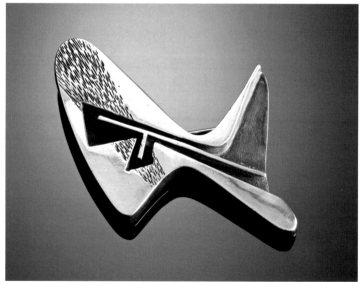

FIGURE 7 [UPPER LEFT]
Margaret De Patta
Sketch for production pin #22,
c. 1947
graphite on paper
5 x 6 in. (12.7 x 15.2 cm)
Margaret De Patta Archives,
Bielawski Trust, Point Richmond,
California

FIGURE 8 [UPPER RIGHT]
Margaret De Patta
Production pin #22,
designed 1947, produced 1947–57
sterling silver, quartz
1⅞ x 3¼ x ¾ in.
(48 x 83 x 19 mm)
Montreal Museum of Fine Arts,
Liliane and David M. Stewart
Collection, Gift of Paul Leblanc

FIGURE 9 [LOWER LEFT]
Margaret De Patta
Sketch for production pin #15,
c. 1947
graphite on paper
4 x 8⅛ in. (10.2 x 20.6 cm)
Margaret De Patta Archives,
Bielawski Trust, Point Richmond,
California

FIGURE 10 [LOWER RIGHT]
Margaret De Patta
Production pin #15,
designed 1947, produced 1947–57
sterling silver
2½ x 2½ x ½ in. (64 x 64 x 13 mm)
Collection of the Oakland Museum
of California, Gift of Jan Gregory in
memory of Mildred Rosenthal

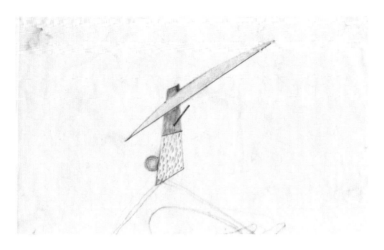

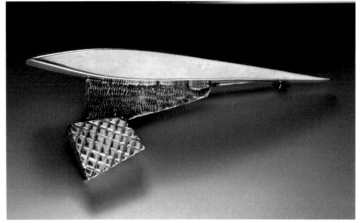

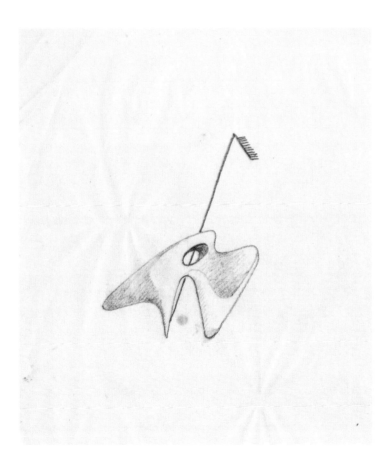

FIGURE 11 [UPPER LEFT]
Margaret De Patta
Sketch for production pin #5, c. 1945
graphite on paper
4¼ x 7 in. (10.8 x 17.8 cm)
Margaret De Patta Archives, Bielawski Trust,
Point Richmond, California

FIGURE 12 [UPPER RIGHT]
Margaret De Patta
Production pin #5,
designed 1944, produced 1946–57
sterling silver
1¼ x 3 x ⅝ in. (32 x 76 x 16 mm)
Montreal Museum of Fine Arts,
Liliane and David M. Stewart Collection,
Gift of Paul Leblanc

FIGURE 13 [LOWER LEFT]
Margaret De Patta
Sketch for production pin #4, c. 1944
graphite on paper
7¼ x 8⅛ in. (18.4 x 20.6 cm)
Margaret De Patta Archives, Bielawski Trust,
Point Richmond, California

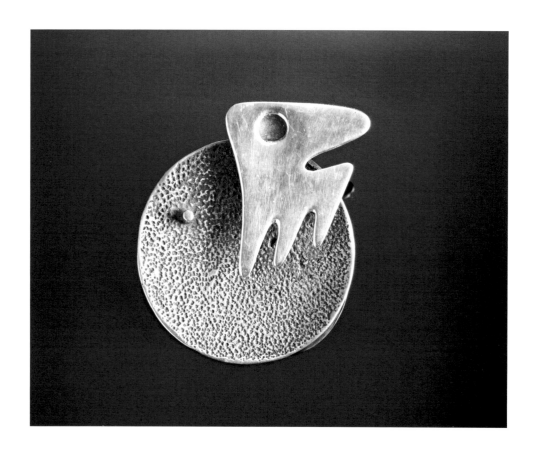

FIGURE 14
Margaret De Patta
Production pin #10 (Running Ghost),
designed 1947, produced 1947–57
sterling silver
2⅛ x 1⅞ x ½ in. (54 x 48 x 13 mm)
Private collection

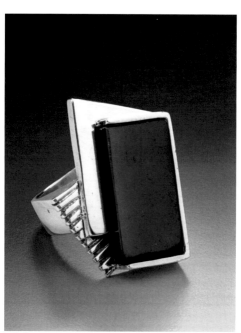

FIGURE 15 [FAR LEFT]
Margaret De Patta
Production ring #1,
designed 1942, produced 1946–57
sterling silver, quartz
1 x ⅞ x ⅜ in. (25 x 22 x 10 mm)
Collection of Forrest L. Merrill

FIGURE 16 [LEFT]
Margaret De Patta
Production ring #8,
designed 1944, produced 1946–57
sterling silver, jade
1 x 1⅛ x 1 in. (25 x 29 x 25 mm)
Montreal Museum of Fine Arts,
Liliane and David M. Stewart Collection,
Gift of Paul Leblanc

FIGURE 17 [LEFT]
Margaret De Patta
Production ring #30,
designed 1945, produced 1946–57
sterling silver
1⅛ x 1 x ¾ in. (29 x 25 x 19 mm)
Tacoma Art Museum, Gift of Ron Ho
in honor of Ramona Solberg

FIGURE 18 [RIGHT]
Margaret De Patta
Production ring #21,
designed 1947, produced 1947–57
sterling silver
⅞ x ⅞ x 1¾ in. (22 x 22 x 45 mm)
Tacoma Art Museum, Gift of Mary Davis

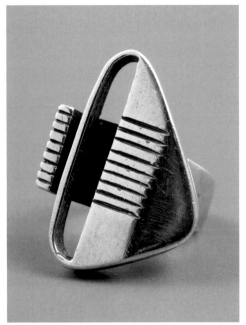

FIGURE 19
Margaret De Patta
Production ring #3,
designed 1944, produced 1946–57
sterling silver
⅝ x 1 x 1⅛ in. (16 x 25 x 29 mm)
Museum of Fine Arts, Boston,
The Daphne Farago Collection

With so many prestigious outlets, Designs Contemporary appeared to be off to a promising start, but in reality, sales were slow. Correspondence with multiple retailers outlines a distinct pattern: initial high enthusiasm for the designs, followed by few sales, and eventually the discontinuance and return of the consignment. Nevertheless, De Patta was smart enough—and strong-willed enough—to put on a public front, avidly supporting the production line and even boasting of its success. One report cited her making as many as sixty-five copies of each design,[16] and as late as 1962 De Patta claimed in an interview, ". . . shops [were] eager to buy." She emphasized the point by stating, "Soon [it] developed into such a large business, [we] were in competition with Hickok [a major manufacturer of men's jewelry based in Rochester, New York]."[17]

Records clearly indicate that despite lagging sales in production jewelry, sales of commissioned Originals kept the couple financially afloat. "Conditions here in San Francisco are showing considerable signs of economic pressures," Bielawski reported to a retailer in 1949. "Strangely enough—it has affected our little business in an unusual way—the production design sales have fallen off to nil—but Margaret's handmade orders have kept her quite busy—fortunately."[18] In December of the following year, Bielawski again admitted to slow production sales.[19] On their 1950 taxes, however, the Bielawskis reported a business profit of $4,878 ($47,649 in constant dollars).[20] One must conclude from these statements that most of this income came from the sale of Originals.

De Patta and Bielawski attempted to promote the Designs Contemporary line in a variety of ways, even producing an attractive brochure in 1949 with photographs of select designs (fig. 20).

The brochure was sold to retailers who carried the line, mailed gratis to dozens of potential new venues across the country, and sent as a follow-up to inquiries about the jewelry.[21] Despite its widespread use, De Patta reported in 1950 that it generated no sales.[22] A few years later, in 1953, Designs Contemporary made one more, and perhaps the most targeted, attempt at direct marketing, in the form of an introductory special on new wedding band designs. The offer was mailed to a list of national modernist galleries that had appeared in the winter 1950 issue of the Walker Art Center's *Everyday Art Quarterly,* as well as to twenty-nine additional galleries that De Patta and Bielawski identified from other sources.[23] This promotion met with better success, and wedding bands soon became Designs Contemporary's top sellers.[24]

Central to their marketing plan was a retrospective exhibition of De Patta's Originals, complete with jewelry, photographs, and poster boards (fig. 21). Culled from her personal collection of work kept from her earliest days as an art jeweler,[25] the exhibition was offered to new retail outlets for display in their shops. While the exhibition was little more than a display of De Patta's jewelry, calling it a traveling retrospective provided the news hook it needed to gain coverage from local newspapers and radio stations—free exposure that effectively introduced her innovative designs to a new market.

In fact, De Patta rarely paid for advertising. Budget restrictions limited what she could afford, and the only paid ads she ran appeared intermittently in *Arts & Architecture* between 1948 and 1950 (fig. 23). Despite directing three hundred dollars of her 1948 budget toward advertising, and despite receiving a discounted rate of fifteen dollars per month from *Arts & Architecture,* De Patta

FIGURE 20
Brochure for Designs Contemporary production line,
1949
8⅛ x 8⅛ in. (20.6 x 20.6 cm)
Collection of the Oakland Museum of California,
The Margaret De Patta Archive

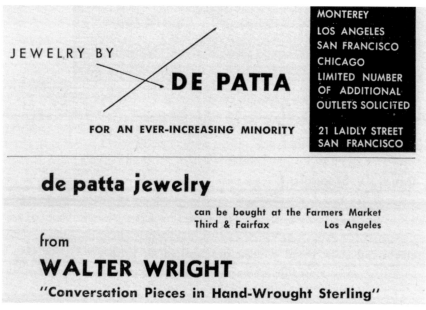

FIGURE 21 [UPPER LEFT]

Installation of Margaret De Patta "retrospective" exhibition at Pacific Shop in San Francisco, 1950
Margaret De Patta Archives, Bielawski Trust, Point Richmond, California

FIGURE 22 [UPPER RIGHT]

Advertisement for jewelry by Margaret De Patta, New Yorker, September 25, 1948
Courtesy of Black, Starr & Frost

FIGURE 23

Advertisement for jewelry by Margaret De Patta, Arts & Architecture, July 1947

ran ads in only three issues that year. Their situation appears to have worsened the following year.[26] In a letter dated October 4, 1949, Bielawski writes, "In spite of the fact that we would like to advertise consistently in *Arts & Architecture* we find ourselves unable to consider [it]. . . . If we have another period as the one just past—we may be selling apples. Rest assured, our thoughts are always with you and as soon as finances allow, our advertising plans."[27] An exchange ensues in which advertising manager Robert Cron writes back, "Damnitall, send us a [*sic*] copy for a 1/16-page and we will carry it for you gratis each month until you are in a position to use regular space."[28] Bielawski agreed to a six-month trial, but pridefully insisted on paying $17.50 per month, stating, "If worse gets more that way—we'll pay off with melted sterling silver, then A&A can get into the jewelry business too."[29] Designs Contemporary's ad appears intermittently in only four issues after this exchange, suggesting the jewelry business continued to struggle financially.[30] Other advertising was placed and paid for by the retail establishments selling De Patta's jewelry. The prestigious New York jeweler Black, Starr & Gorham, for example, opted not to present De Patta's promotional retrospective exhibition, but instead ran a prominent ad for her work in the September 25, 1948, issue of the *New Yorker* (fig. 22). The following month, Mermod, Jaccard & King Jewelry Company placed a similar ad in the *New Yorker*.[31] Other retailers, including Nanny's in San Francisco and Walter Wright in Los Angeles, also featured De Patta's name and jewelry in their advertising.

De Patta discontinued the production line in 1957, claiming marketing it was taking too much of her time and she wanted to concentrate on design.[32] While this is likely true, the low profit margin certainly would have been a factor in this decision. Why did the production line fail as De Patta Originals grew in popularity? The answer lies in De Patta's flawed assumptions concerning price, demand, and market.

De Patta started her line in 1946, amid the growing consumerism of postwar America. After wartime price controls were lifted, the country was faced with rampant inflation, and economists encouraged consumption as the best way to boost the lagging economy.[33] During the years the line was in production, the national gross domestic product (GDP) doubled, and per capita income increased by 35 percent.[34] Also during this period, the number of salaried employees grew by 61 percent, and a strong labor movement led to improvements in factory working conditions and higher wages. By the time Designs Contemporary ceased production, nearly 60 percent of the U.S. population made what was considered a middle-class income.[35] In short, the typical postwar consumer was married, middle class, owned his own home, made more money than his prewar counterpart, and spent like never before.

Given the favorable economic climate and the fact that affordability was De Patta's main motivation for starting the production line, price would seem not to have been a factor in the line's failure to thrive. A letter from Boyd Britton manager Mary MacConnel explained otherwise: "Although numerous customers are interested in your pins, they react quite the opposite when quoted the prices. . . ." Going on to explain just how difficult the situation was, she wrote, "There are those who further criticize the prices as they believe your jewelry to be machinery made at this point."[36] Other retailers echoed this response. Letter after letter voiced concerns such as "Our customers thought they were beautiful . . . but the price. . . ."[37]

While Americans had more money to spend after the war, luxury items such as jewelry were not their priority. In fact, most Americans spent only 1.5 percent of their income on miscellaneous and luxury goods.[38] Instead, they were nesting. They purchased houses at an unprecedented rate[39] and bought furniture and household appliances to turn them into comfortable homes. In the first five years following the war, sales of furniture and household appliances jumped an amazing 240 percent.[40]

Ironically, while De Patta and Bielawski had succeeded in marketing the Designs Contemporary line to galleries and retail establishments that catered to design-savvy consumers, the production jewelry failed to meet the customers' needs for value. Between the inherent limitations of lost-wax casting and De Patta's and Bielawski's desire to keep prices low, most of the production line pieces were both technically and conceptually simple and lacked the innovative design elements that made her Originals so unique. Most pieces were cast in sterling, not gold,[41] and when stones were used, they were cabochons, not intricate opticuts.[42] Yet for the average retail price of $30 ($293 in constant dollars),[43] the customer expected more. Sears, Roebuck and Company and Montgomery Ward sold 14-karat gold rings with semiprecious stones akin to De Patta's for half that price. To put this price further into perspective, for $34, the "modern" housewife could buy a dining table designed by Charles and Ray Eames whose size and

practicality made it a better value than a $30 brooch she thought to be machine made. Because De Patta's jewelry was often sold in stores that carried modern furnishings and housewares, such a comparison could easily have been made.

But price was not the only reason for low sales. Even in upscale Beverly Hills, home to wealthy moguls and movie stars, sales were minimal. Despite a prominent location on the corner of Rodeo Drive and Santa Monica Boulevard, the Van Keppel-Green store carried Designs Contemporary's line for barely a year, between 1949 and 1950. Consigned merchandise was eventually returned with the manager stating, "We have had it in a case directly in the window all the time, and, although we have had many inquiries about it and shown it to a lot of people, we haven't been able to culminate a sale."[44]

De Patta's jewelry consistently failed to attract a mass market. The consumer that she worked so hard to supply with high-quality design at an affordable price was simply not interested in avant-garde design. This was dicovered time and time again as postwar marketers studied new ways to increase sales.[45] Most middle-class Americans rejected the modernist mantra "less is more" in favor of "more is better," and in response to that sentiment manufacturers and industrial designers created large-finned automobiles and heavily-chromed refrigerators.[46]

Had she been less idealistic, De Patta might have learned this lesson as early as the 1940s. Around the time the production line started, she experimented with low-priced "trinket" jewelry for a friend's variety store. Punched out of inexpensive pot metal, these pieces were priced at around one dollar each (fig. 24). "It

was a beautiful design . . . ," recalled the store owner, "[but] we never sold a piece."[47] Some time later, she attempted a similar strategy with her #7 production ring (fig. 25), which she produced cheaply with matching earrings in hopes of marketing them to a department store (fig. 26). These pieces do not seem to have gone into full production,[48] and De Patta later admitted that, from a market standpoint, retailers were justified in not buying them.[49] Though innovative and unique, her designs could not be appreciated by the typical consumer. As designer Edward S. Evans, Jr., wrote, "Modern design labeled 'For the world of tomorrow' was instead 'Too new for the world today.'"[50]

De Patta's innovative designs appealed only to a select group—typically artists, academics, and educated, upper-middle-class professionals who were "esthetically aware, intellectually inclined and politically progressive."[51] She shared a kinship with them, further developing their relationship through her working process. With each commission, she asked the client to answer a questionnaire asking about such desired tangibles as preferred metals and stones and ring size, as well as details that would personalize the design and make it unique. Such questions included preferences for angular or curved elements, personal style, and whether the piece was for constant wear or occasional use. This personal interaction likely helped sway new clients who previously had not had a proclivity for modern design. Unfortunately, this interaction did not exist in the development of production designs, a factor that may have cost De Patta new additions to her "ever-increasing minority."

Yet De Patta remained undeterred, and she was not alone in her idealism. Electing themselves as educators, De Patta, along with other designers, retailers, and cultural ambassadors attempted to elevate consumers' taste. Exhibition series such as *Good Design* (organized by the Museum of Modern Art between 1949 and 1955) and *California Design* (organized triennially by the Pasadena Art Museum between 1955 and 1984) were the largest and most successful of these attempts, although historians have varied opinions on the amount of influence these efforts had on consumers' taste. While many agree that *Good Design* raised awareness levels and promoted sales of many of the useful objects that were featured, the program's main audience consisted of members of the upper middle class with sophisticated predilections. The remainder of America still preferred over-stuffed sofas to Eames lounge chairs.[52]

While De Patta established her name among design-sensitive consumers, she failed to establish herself beyond this elite group, thus failing to expand her market. The support of *Good Design* or the more regional *California Design* exhibitions could have helped her overcome some of these obstacles; both exhibitions heavily promoted their designers, granting some of them semi-celebrity status. Middle-class Americans may not have liked the Eames LCW (Lounge Chair, Wood), but they more than likely had seen it and were familiar with the name Charles Eames through publications such as *Life* magazine, which

often featured images of modern products and the idealized American lifestyle. Unfortunately, De Patta was not eligible for either exhibition. *Good Design* featured "useful objects," a category its jurors did not feel included jewelry, and the *California Design* program was ill timed for De Patta's advantage. In its early years, *California Design* focused solely on southern California designers and did not even include jewelry until 1965, a year after De Patta's death.

De Patta's coveted "ever-increasing minority" was in reality never increasing. A cluster of creative intellectuals remained loyal to her, but attempts to expand her market beyond this group yielded little fruit. In time, education would reap changes in the art jewelry market, but not quickly enough to help De Patta. She accepted the failure of her production attempts, yet maintained her vision for the future, stating: "I look forward to the time when the designer will work with [the] production method—when design will influence the methods of production and the means of production will in turn influence the design. Production will someday be utilized for 'quality' rather than 'cheapness.'"[53]

FIGURE 25
Margaret De Patta
Production ring #7, designed 1946,
produced 1946–57
sterling silver, pearl
1¼ x ¾ x 1⅛ in. (32 x 19 x 29 mm)
Museum of Arts and Design, New York, Gift of
Eugene Bielawski, The Margaret De Patta Bequest,
through the American Craft Council, 1976

FIGURE 26
Margaret De Patta
Trinket ring, reproduction of production ring #7,
c. 1947
mixed materials
1 x ¾ x ⅞ in. (25 x 19 x 22 mm)
Margaret De Patta Archives, Bielawski Trust,
Point Richmond, California

125

1

Handwritten draft of unpublished essay titled "Good Design" by De Patta, c. 1962–64, Margaret De Patta Archives, Bielawski Trust, Point Richmond, California.

2

Production pieces were handmade using the lost-wax method of casting. Once cast, each piece was finished by hand. Peter Macchiarini felt that true art could not be mass-produced and often spoke out on the subject. He was one of several colleagues who felt that De Patta had sold out when she began her production line.

3

Margaret De Patta, "De Patta," *Arts & Architecture* 64, no. 7 (July 1947): 30.

4

The Designs Contemporary business name was used inconsistently. It first appears in records on account receipts after December 1947, a year after the production line began. Prior to this, De Patta had marketed and sold her ware under the label Jewelry by De Patta. These two business names were used interchangeably by De Patta, and later by Bielawski, throughout the second half of the twentieth century. De Patta and Bielawski continued to use the Designs Contemporary name on stationery and receipts after the line was discontinued in 1957. This is likely the result of conservation and the costs of reprinting rather than a distinct business decision. However, Bielawski also used the business name in written appraisals made after De Patta's death, even to the extent of handwriting the name above his signature on the appraisal reports. Clearly Bielawski associated the Designs Contemporary name with any business relating to De Patta's work, not strictly limited to the production line. The last known appraisal using the Designs Contemporary name is dated 1991. Margaret De Patta Archives, Bielawski Trust, Point Richmond, California.

5

This phrase first appeared in the 1947 *Arts & Architecture* article. It was at times used as the Designs Contemporary tag line, though inconsistently.

6

California Legislature, *Fourth Report of the Senate Fact-Finding Committee on Un-American Activities: Communist Front Organizations* (California State Senate, 1948), 51, 53.

7

Michael Elkins, *Arts & Architecture* 62, no. 8 (August 1945): 30, 31, 55. I am indebted to Martha Bielawski for bringing this article to my attention.

8

Artist Merry Renk, interview by the author, 11 March 2009, San Francisco, California. Only in 1956 did De Patta finally admit openly that the artist-designer "is not temperamentally adapted to the personal handling of repetitious production." Quoted in Don Wallance, *Shaping America's Products* (New York: Reinhold Publishing, 1956), 165. The original source of this quote is unknown, although this sentiment is expressed again in De Patta's article "From the Inside," *The Palette* 32, no. 2 (spring 1952): 14–19.

9

Earring and cuff link designs could be made in either format depending on the buyer's needs.

10

Unsigned letter to Moderntrend gallery, San Rafael, California, 22 May 1953, Margaret De Patta archives, Bielawski Trust, Point Richmond, California. The promotion included wedding bands in fifteen different designs.

11

De Patta had numbered her work prior to the production line. However, the production line generated a definitive, though confusing, numbering system that distinguished between the production pieces, one-of-a-kind "Originals," and permanent collection items.

12

Margaret De Patta Archives, Bielawski Trust, Point Richmond, California. It is unclear how De Patta defined "exclusive territory" since she at times had multiple retailers in the same city.

13

For drafts of these purchasing policies, see the Margaret De Patta Archives, Bielawski Trust, Point Richmond, California, and the Margaret De Patta Papers, Archives of American Art, Smithsonian Institution. It is interesting to note that these drafts are mostly written in Bielawski's handwriting, suggesting that he managed most of the business dealings.

14

Known outlets include 750 Studio (Chicago), Amberg-Hirth (San Francisco), Black Starr & Gorham (New York), Boyd, Britton Association (Chicago), Cabaniss (Denver), Cargoes (San Francisco), Cele Peterson (Tucson), Contemporary House (Dallas), Crossroads (Portland, Oregon), Design Today (Lubbock, Texas), Hughes Gallery (Houston), IFA Galleries (Washington, D. C.), Leonard Linn (Winnetka, Illinois), Modern Center (Minneapolis, Minnesota), Nanny's Design Gallery (San Francisco), Pacific Shop (San Francisco), Ted Herreid (Tacoma, Washington), Treasure Chest (Memphis, Tennessee), Modern House (Midland, Texas), Zacho's (Los Angeles Farmers Market).

15

Starting in 1947, De Patta stamped the word "Originals" on her handmade studio jewelry to distinguish it from production pieces. Due to space constraints, the stamp was used inconsistently and after 1950, rarely.

16

Wallance, *Shaping America's Products*, 165.

17

"Margaret De Patta," Notes, 7 May 1962. Yoshiko Uchida papers, BANC MSS 86/97c, The Bancroft Library, University of California, Berkeley. Box 45, folder 13.

18

Bielawski to Brewer, 6 June 1949, Margaret De Patta Archives, Bielawski Trust, Point Richmond, California.

19

Bielawski to Robert Gottschalk, 12 December 1950, Margaret De Patta Archives, Bielawski Trust, Point Richmond, California.

20

1950 California individual income tax filing for Margaret De Patta Bielawski and Eugene Bielawski, Margaret De Patta Archives, Bielawski Trust, Point Richmond, California.

21

In an unsigned form letter dated 11 October 1949, Designs Contemporary suggested retailers mail the brochure to their existing clientele. Brochures were sold for $8.50 for one hundred pieces. Margaret De Patta Archives, Bielawski Trust, Point Richmond, California.

22

De Patta to Robert Cron, 10 March 1950, Margaret De Patta Archives, Bielawski Trust, Point Richmond, California.

23

"Where to Buy," *Everyday Art Quarterly* 17 (winter 1950–51): 12. Margaret De Patta Archives, Bielawski Trust, Point Richmond, California.

24

Margaret De Patta Papers, Archives of American Art, Smithsonian Institution. Ring sales data based on an assessment of receipts and orders in the Margaret De Patta Archives, Bielawski Trust, Point Richmond, California.

25

By the time of her death, the permanent collection totaled over two hundred objects. Eugene Bielawski donated a large selection of these pieces to the Oakland Museum of California in 1967 and 1968, forming the Margaret De Patta Memorial Collection.

26
1948 budget, Margaret De Patta Papers, Archives of American Art, Smithsonian Institution. For information on the discounted rate, see Robert Cron to De Patta, 4 June 1947, Margaret De Patta Archives, Bielawski Trust, Point Richmond, California. The 1948 *Arts & Architecture* advertisements ran in the January, February, and March issues. It is unknown when De Patta drafted the budget dated 1948, but interestingly, in a letter dated 15 January 1948, *Arts & Architecture* acknowledged the request to stop printing the ad (Ruth Gerson to Bielawski, 15 January 1948, Margaret De Patta Archives, Bielawski Trust, Point Richmond, California).

27
Bielawski to Cron, 4 October 1949, Margaret De Patta Archives, Bielawski Trust, Point Richmond, California.

28
Cron to Bielawski, 13 October 1949, Margaret De Patta Archives, Bielawski Trust, Point Richmond, California.

29
Bielawski to Cron, 17 October 1949, Margaret De Patta Archives, Bielawski Trust, Point Richmond, California.

30
The four issues in which advertisements appear are December 1949, March 1950, May 1950, and June 1950.

31
New Yorker, 2 October 1948, 93.

32
Yoshiko Uchida papers, BANC MSS 86/97c, The Bancroft Library, University of California, Berkeley.

33
"Good Times a-Comin'," *Life* 49, no. 18 (5 May 1947): 30.

34
Lizabeth Cohen, *A Consumer's Republic: The Politics of Mass Consumption in Postwar America* (New York: Alfred A. Knopf, 2003), 121. Stephanie Coontz, *The Way We Never Were: American Families and the Nostalgia Trap* (New York: Basic Books, 1992), 24.

35
Coontz, ibid.

36
Mary MacConnel to Margaret De Patta, 3 December 1949, Margaret De Patta Archives, Bielawski Trust, Point Richmond, California.

37
Quepha Rawls, Design Today, Lubbock, Texas, to De Patta, n.d., Margaret De Patta Archives, Bielawski Trust, Point Richmond, California.

38
James P. Mitchell, *How American Buying Habits Change* (Washington, D.C.: U.S. Department of Labor, 1959), 50.

39
In the postwar housing boom between 1945 and 1960, single-family home ownership jumped from forty-two percent to sixty-two percent.

40
Coontz, *The Way We Never Were*, 25.

41
Some pieces, particularly wedding bands, were offered in gold or with gold elements for a higher price.

42
An exception to this is production ring #1, which used a lens-cut crystal. Though not as complex as other opticuts, this ring was one of her more expensive production pieces, retailing at $42.50.

43
"Constant dollars" refers here to the value of the dollar in 2011.

44
Brewer to De Patta, 2 February 1950, Margaret De Patta Archives, Bielawski Trust, Point Richmond, California.

45
In the 1950s, retailers became interested in motivational marketing as they studied the psychological reasons behind consumer choices. For an account of this research, see Pierre Martineau, *Motivation in Advertising: Motives That Make People Buy* (New York: McGraw Hill, 1957).

46
Shelly Nickles, "More Is Better: Mass Consumption, Gender, and Class Identity in Postwar America," *American Quarterly* 54, no. 4 (December 2002): 582. See also, Raymond Loewy, *Never Leave Well Enough Alone* (New York: Simon and Schuster, 1951), 221–22, 277-83.

47
Avis Blanchette, interview by author, 21 June 2010, Point Richmond, California.

48
According to friends close to the Bielawskis, this ring and earring set was being prototyped for Sears, Roebuck and Company or Montgomery Ward, however a search of the two retailers' catalogs between the years 1946 and 1957 did not find such items listed.

49
Wallance, *Shaping America's Products*, 165.

50
Edward S. Evans, Jr., "The Manufacturer's Position," in *Good Design Is Your Business* (Buffalo, N. Y.: Buffalo Fine Art Academy, 1947), 29.

51
Dr. Blanche R. Brown, "Ed Wiener to Me," in *Jewelry by Ed Wiener*, exhibition catalogue (New York: Fifty-50 Gallery, 1988), 13. While Brown is discussing Wiener, De Patta's clients—many of whom fit this description—likely felt the same way.

52
Peter Dormer, *Design Since 1945* (Philadelphia: Philadelphia Museum of Art, 1983), 235; Richard Horn, "MoMA's 'Good Design' Programs Changed Historic U.S. Taste," *Industrial Design* 29, no. 2 (March/April 1982), 43–47; Terence Riley and Edward Eigen, "Between the Museum and the Marketplace: Selling Good Design," in *The Museum of Modern Art at Mid-Century: At Home and Abroad* (New York: Museum of Modern Art, 1994), 151–77.

53
Handwritten draft of an unpublished essay titled "Good Design" by De Patta, c. 1962–1964, Margaret De Patta Archives, Bielawski Trust, Point Richmond, California.åå

Timeline and **Bibliography**

Timeline and Selected Exhibition History

EARLY YEARS

1903

Mary Margaret Strong is born on March 18 in Tacoma, Washington, to Harold Meade Strong (born July 9, 1879, Waverly, Iowa) and Mary Margaret Loska (born August 5, 1883, Austria).

The Strong family resides at 1409 South G Street, Tacoma, Washington.

1904

Margaret's sister Adelia Frances Strong is born on May 3.

1904–1906

The Strong family resides at 1742 South E Street, Tacoma, Washington.

1910–1915

The Strong family moves to San Diego, California, and resides at 1651 Second Street, in the neighborhood known as Banker's Hill.

Harold works as a janitor at San Diego High School.

1911–1922

Harold works as a deputy city assessor.

1912

Margaret's sister Charlotte Pauline Strong is born on October 22.

1916–1923

The Strong family resides at 1667 Second Street, San Diego, California.

1917–1921

Margaret attends and graduates from San Diego High School.

ART TRAINING AND EDUCATION

1921–1923

Margaret studies painting at the newly opened San Diego Academy of Fine Arts in the old Sacramento Building in Balboa Park. The short-lived institution closed during World War II when the U.S. military occupied the building.

1922

Margaret marries Floyd Charlous Bollman, a bank teller, in San Diego on January 16.

1924

Floyd Charlous Bollman dies of tuberculosis.

1923–1925

Margaret studies painting at the California School of Fine Arts in San Francisco.

1925

Margaret marries her second husband, William Schuster, in Sacramento, California, on February 14.

1927

Margaret and William divorce on September 28.

1928

Margaret's father, Harold, marries his second wife, Elizabeth Carolyn Blauvelt, in San Diego. Margaret's half-brother, Harold, is born January 26, 1935.

Margaret's mother, Mary, eventually resides in Oakland.

FIGURE 1
Margaret Strong, senior yearbook photo, San Diego High School, 1921

FIGURE 2
Margaret De Patta
Untitled, c. 1917–21
gouache on paper
16½ x 11½ in. (41.9 x 29.2 cm)
Margaret De Patta Archives, Bielawski Trust, Point Richmond, California

Margaret receives a scholarship from the Art Students League in New York and registers for Kenneth Hayes Miller's life drawing class and William von Schlegell's life drawing class beginning in October. She cancels her registration, perhaps in anticipation of her pending nuptials.

Margaret marries her third husband, Salvatore (Sam) De Patta, a salesman of Venezuelan descent, in Napa, California, on October 6.

1929
Frustrated by the lack of creativity in traditional wedding rings, Margaret begins studying basic jewelry design in San Francisco, apprenticing herself to Armenian jeweler Armin Hairenian at the Art Copper Shop, so she can make her own ring.

Margaret attends the Art Students League in New York. She takes a month-long class in painting taught by Kenneth Hayes Miller.

1932
Margaret begins studying enameling and engraving in San Francisco.

1935
Margaret starts working professionally and opens a small workshop in her San Francisco home.

Margaret begins selling her work through Amberg-Hirth, a craft gallery in San Francisco. Records indicate she exhibited with them through 1946. Amberg-Hirth closes in 1954.

Margaret participates in the California Pacific International Exposition in San Diego. She exhibits a pendant, chain bracelet, and a few rings.

1936
Margaret and Sam De Patta purchase a house at 21 Laidley Street in San Francisco.

Margaret and Sam travel to Mexico in February. She takes photographs and keeps a journal of their month-long trip.

1939
Margaret and Sam travel across the country to New York City to attend the World's Fair.

1939–1940
Margaret participates in the Golden Gate International Exposition in San Francisco. Her works are showcased in the Decorative Arts section under *Modern Silver* (holloware) and *Modern Jewelry* (brooch) at Treasure Island and in the Metalwork and Woodworking section *Artists and Craftsmen in Action* at the Palace of Fine Arts. Work by European modernist László Moholy-Nagy (Margaret's future mentor) is exhibited under *Miscellaneous*.

Margaret begins an artistic collaboration with Francis Sperisen, self-taught lapidary in San Francisco. Many Bay Area jewelers work with Sperisen, including Merry Renk, Florence Resnikoff, and Irena Brynner.

FIGURE 3
Margaret De Patta in studio, 1939
Margaret De Patta Archives, Bielawski Trust,
Point Richmond, California

FIGURE 4
*The New Bauhaus American
School of Design catalogue,* 1938
Margaret De Patta Archives, Bielawski Trust,
Point Richmond, California

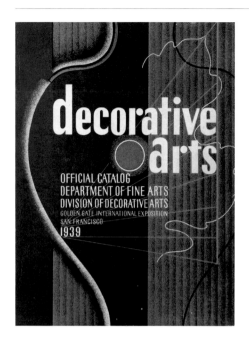

1940–1941
Margaret attends Moholy-Nagy's School of Design in Chicago. During her time in school, Margaret studies photography and sculpture. She meets Eugene Bielawski, an industrial designer and instructor at the school.

1941
Margaret and Sam divorce on August 29. She remodels the Laidley Street house following her divorce.

MID-CAREER

1944
Margaret participates in a group exhibition at the California Palace of the Legion of Honor in San Francisco with silversmiths Antonio Pineda and Franz Bergmann, May 4–31.

1944–1947
Margaret teaches at the Tom Mooney Labor School (known later as the California Labor School). Classes include modern design for small crafts, experimental stage design, basic design workshop, home planning, plastics, industrial art seminars, and sculpture.

1940
Margaret attends a summer course at Mills College taught by László Moholy-Nagy, guest artist, director, and founder of the New Bauhaus (which became the School of Design in 1938, the Institute of Design in 1944, and part of Illinois Institute of Technology in 1949). Additional faculty from Chicago include photographer and painter György Kepes, weaver Marli Ehrman, and furniture designer Charles Niedringhaus, among others. Classes are taught in conjunction with the Museum of Modern Art's traveling exhibition *The Bauhaus: How It Worked*. Courses include drawing, painting, photography, weaving, paper cutting, metalwork, modeling, and casting.

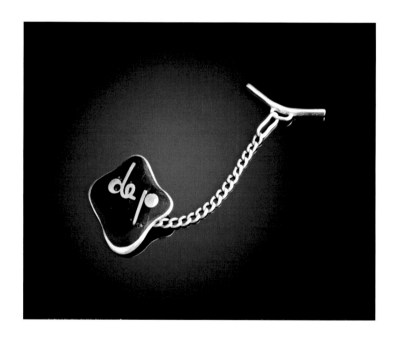

FIGURE 5
Official Catalog, Department of Fine Arts,
Division of Decorative Arts, Golden Gate
International Exposition, San Francisco, 1939
Margaret De Patta Archives, Bielawski Trust,
Point Richmond, California

FIGURE 6
Margaret De Patta
Key chain, c. 1939
sterling silver
1¼ x 1⅛ in., chain 5⅞ in.
(32 x 29 mm, chain 149 mm)
Collection of Steven Cabella

Margaret and Eugene purchase thirty acres on Hein Road in Napa, California, with the intention of establishing an artists' cooperative school of contemporary design with jewelers Franz Bergmann and Gerhard Becker. Their school never opened.

Margaret marries Eugene Bielawski, her fourth husband, on December 26.

1947
Margaret teaches a summer session at the Shattuck School and Portland Art Museum in Portland, Oregon, sponsored by Portland Public Schools, the Ceramic Studio, the University of Oregon, and the Portland Art Museum.

Eugene Bielawski arrives in San Francisco in June 1945 to serve as director of arts at the California Labor School.

Margaret becomes chairman of the Basic Design Workshop at the California Labor School, where she conducts classes in basic design, stage design, and sculpture. Art department colleagues include sculptor and jeweler Peter Macchiarini, sculptor and jeweler Claire Falkenstein, ceramist Edith Heath, sculptor Freda Koblick, painter Louise Gilbert, illustrator and painter Giacomo Patri, graphic artist Adelyne Cross, and muralist Victor Arnautoff. Due to charges of un-American and Communist activities the school eventually closes in 1957. De Patta, Macchiarini, and Bielawski are all blacklisted in the 1947 and 1949 reports published by the Senate of the State of California.

1946
Margaret participates in the Museum of Modern Art's landmark group traveling exhibition *Modern Handmade Jewelry,* in New York City, September 17–November 17. The exhibition features 147 pieces of jewelry made by twenty-five artists, sculptors, and studio jewelers, including Anni Albers, Ward Bennett, Alexander Calder, Jacques Lipschitz, Julio De Diego, Paul Lobel, Richard Pousette-Dart, among others. Margaret shows three rings and a pin.

Margaret and Eugene start a limited edition production line in their San Francisco home studio in order to produce handcrafted jewelry for under fifty dollars. They begin working under the company name Designs Contemporary as early as 1947.

FIGURE 9
Margaret De Patta and **Eugene Bielawski**
Holiday greeting cards, 1940–54
mixed media
4½ x 6½ in. (11.4 x 16.5 cm), average size
Margaret De Patta Archives, Bielawski Trust, Point Richmond, California

FIGURE 10
Milton Halberstadt
(1919–2000)
Margaret De Patta, 1947
Margaret De Patta Archives, Bielawski Trust, Point Richmond, California

Margaret organizes the exhibition *New Approach in Art Education and Jewelry by dePatta* [sic] at the Oregon Ceramic Studio in July. Work includes a representation of Margaret's jewelry, as well as work by her students from the California Labor School.

Margaret's essay "Jewelry for An Ever Increasing Minority" is published under the title "De Patta" in *Arts & Architecture*, July 1947.

1948

Margaret participates in the group exhibition *Modern Jewelry Under Fifty Dollars* at the Walker Art Center in Minneapolis, Minnesota. Thirty-two artists, including Claire Falkenstein, Bob Winston, Sam Kramer, Paul Lobel, Art Smith, and Harry Bertoia, among others, exhibit 282 pieces of jewelry. Margaret exhibits nine rings and four pins from her production line.

1949

Margaret participates in the show *An Exhibition for Modern Living* at the Detroit Institute of Arts in Michigan, September 11–November 20. She shows a ring and a set of earrings.

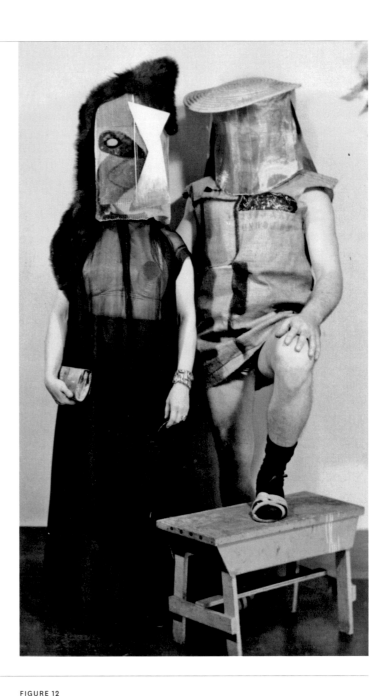

FIGURE 11
Margaret De Patta
De Patta Originals, c. 1949
black-and-white photograph
7¼ x 8¼ in. (18.4 x 21 cm)
Margaret De Patta Archives, Bielawski Trust,
Point Richmond, California

FIGURE 12
Margaret De Patta and Eugene Bielawski at California Labor School costume party, c. 1948
Margaret De Patta Archives, Bielawski Trust,
Point Richmond, California

LATER CAREER

1950

Margaret participates in the group exhibition *Contemporary American Jewelry* at Oberlin College's Dudley Peter Allen Memorial Art Museum in Oberlin, Ohio. She shows three rings and three pins.

Margaret participates in and sells her jewelry at the Fall Festival, a craft fair at Presidio Hill School, San Francisco, California, alongside jeweler Peter Macchiarini and ceramists Edith Heath and Jade Snow Wong. She puts on consignment ten rings, five pins, and one set of cufflinks.

1951

Margaret and Eugene purchase a home at 1137 Terrace Drive in Napa Valley, California.

Margaret participates in a group exhibition at the Fine Arts Gallery in San Diego, California.

Margaret co-founds the Metal Arts Guild of San Francisco along with Eugene Bielawski, Virginia and Peter Macchiarini, Irena Brynner, Harry Dixon, Merry Renk, Caroline Rosene, Bob Winston, and Franz Bergmann, among others. The guild was formed to create a network of support for emerging and established metal craftspeople, serve the economic interests of its membership, and promote the metal arts through members' participation in local, national, and international exhibitions, traveling shows, and competitions. The Metal Arts Guild still exists today.

Margaret participates in the opening group exhibition featuring Bay Area artists for the new Richmond Art Center in Richmond, California, April 17–May 13. She shows two pins, one set of earrings, and two rings.

Margaret participates in the group exhibition *34 American Artists* at the University Gallery on the University of Minnesota campus in Minneapolis. Thirty-four American artists show textiles, sculpture, ceramics, and jewelry.

Margaret's work is featured in an honorary special exhibition in the Arts and Crafts section for the Los Angeles County Fair Association in Pomona, California. She exhibits two scarabs, two bracelets, thirteen rings, two neckpieces/pendants, two pairs of earrings, four pins, a figure, and six photographs. Margaret also serves as one of five jurors for arts and crafts entries.

Margaret participates in the annual San Francisco Arts Festival sponsored by the San Francisco Art Commission. Venues for the exhibition include the San Francisco Civic Auditorium and the California Palace of the Legion of Honor, among others. Margaret receives a merit award in 1954 and a purchase award in 1960.

1952

Margaret publishes a seminal article, "From the Inside," in *The Palette's* spring journal, produced by the Art Department and Delta Phi Delta at Ball State Teachers College in Muncie, Indiana.

Margaret participates in a group exhibition at the California State Fair Arts & Crafts Exhibit, Allied Arts Guild, in Sacramento, California, October 13–18. She exhibits two rings, one set of earrings, and four pins.

1953

Margaret participates in the landmark traveling exhibition *Designer Craftsmen U.S.A. 1953,* coordinated by the American Craftsmen's Educational Council and sponsored by the Brooklyn Museum in New York, October 22, 1953–January 23, 1954. More than 243 items are exhibited, including metals, ceramics, textiles, and wood. One piece of Margaret's is shown, a pendant made of gold, silver, onyx, and crystal.

1955

Margaret participates in the group exhibition *84 Contemporary Jewelers* at the Walker Art Center in Minneapolis, Minnesota.

Margaret serves as a jury member for craft entries for the art section at the California State Fair and Exposition in Sacramento, California.

Margaret participates in the traveling group exhibition *Creative Jewelry, 1955–1957* at the American Federation of Arts in Racine, Wisconsin. Margaret exhibits twelve pieces of jewelry.

Margaret participates in the traveling group exhibition *American Jewelry and Related Objects,* organized by the Huntington Galleries of Huntington, West Virginia (now the Huntington Museum of Art), and co-sponsored by the Hickok Manufacturing Company of Rochester, New York. Among the pieces she exhibits is a quartz and gold pendant. She receives a merit award.

Margaret's jewelry is featured in a solo exhibition at the Mills College Art Department, Oakland, California. She shows four pins, one ring, and one pendant.

Margaret participates in a group exhibition, the *Annual Invitational Show,* at Iowa State Teachers College (now known as University of Northern Iowa) in Cedar Falls, Iowa, March 10–April 8. The invitational showcases craftsmen in the fields of jewelry, silversmithing, and enamels. She shows one pin and two rings.

Margaret participates in the traveling group exhibition *The Arts in Western Living,* sponsored by the Los Angeles County Fair Association, September 16–October 2. Teams of architects, sculptors, painters, and designer-craftsmen collaborate and produce twenty-three exhibits. An estimated one hundred thousand visitors a day attend.

1956

Margaret begins a long correspondence with her client and friend Adelle Davis, a pioneering nutritionist whose books promoting healthy eating brought her to national attention in the 1950s.

Margaret exhibits her jewelry in a solo exhibition, *Jewelry by Margaret De Patta Bielawski,* in the Ohio Union Lounge at Ohio State University in Columbus, May 27–June 16. Thirty-seven of Margaret's creations are featured, including photographs, neckpieces, figures, bracelets, rings, pins, pendants, and earrings.

Margaret participates in the group exhibition *Craftsmanship in a Changing World,* Museum of Contemporary Crafts (predecessor to the Museum of Arts and Design) in New York, September 20–November 4. Margaret shows one pendant and two rings.

FIGURE 13
Imogen Cunningham (1883–1976)
Portrait of Margaret De Patta with sculpture by Ruth Asawa, 1955
gelatin silver print
8¾ x 5¼ in. (22.2 x 13.3 cm)
Margaret De Patta Archives, Bielawski Trust,
Point Richmond, California

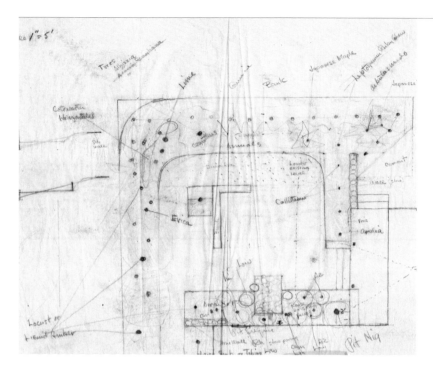

organized by the Metal Arts Guild and circulated by the Western Association of Art Museum Directors.

Margaret and Eugene decide to discontinue their limited edition production line. Margaret focuses strictly on custom orders and experimental work.

1958

Margaret is a panelist for *Vision and Individual Response*, a seminar held in Lake Geneva, Wisconsin, in conjunction with the Second Annual American Craftsmen's Council Conference, *Dimensions of Design*.

Margaret is one of seventy-five American craftsmen selected to exhibit in the American section of *Expo 58: Exposition Universelle et Internationale de Bruxelles*, also known as the Brussels World's Fair. A 14-karat white gold with diamond pendant

Margaret teaches jewelry design during two summer sessions at the California College of Arts and Crafts (now the California College of the Arts) in Oakland, July 9–August 31.

1957

Margaret and Eugene convert their 1137 Terrace Drive, Napa Valley farmhouse into a modern residence.

Margaret attends *Asilomar: The First Annual Conference of American Craftsmen*, sponsored by the American Craftsmen's Council in Asilomar, California.

Margaret participates in the traveling group exhibition *Jewelry, Past and Present* at the Long Beach Museum of Art in Long Beach, California,

FIGURE 14
Margaret De Patta
Landscaping plans for Napa home, c. 1957–62
graphite on paper
10 x 13¾ in. (25.4 x 35.9 cm)
Margaret De Patta Archives, Bielawski Trust,
Point Richmond, California

FIGURE 15
Margaret De Patta and Eugene Bielawski
at home in Napa, c. 1957
Margaret De Patta Archives, Bielawski Trust,
Point Richmond, California

FIGURE 16
Dinner table in Napa home, c. 1957
Margaret De Patta Archives, Bielawski Trust,
Point Richmond, California

is one of the works she exhibits. Irena Brynner and John Paul Miller are among the American jewelers selected.

1959
Margaret receives a commission from Heath Ceramics to develop a ceramics line for the company. The line never went into production. Edith Heath founded Heath Ceramics in the mid-1940s and the company still exists today.

Margaret is one of twenty-five participants at the *Contemporary Jewelry* exhibition held at the Chapman Library Gallery of Milwaukee-Downer College in Milwaukee, Wisconsin. She exhibits two rings and two pendants.

1960
Margaret and Eugene travel to Japan and Hong Kong during the months of October, November, and December.

Margaret participates in the group exhibition *Designer Craftsmen U.S.A. 1960,* organized by the Museum of Contemporary Crafts (the predecessor to the Museum of Arts and Design) in New York, and the American Craftsmen's Council. The exhibition includes one of Margaret's jewelry pieces, a pin made of white gold, onyx, jade, and coral.

Margaret receives a five-hundred-dollar grant to develop her designs for the International Design Competition for Sterling Silver Flatware co-sponsored by the Museum of Contemporary Crafts, the American Craftsmen's Council, and the International Silver Company. Eliminated after the second round, Margaret continued to develop her designs in stainless steel castings for friends.

Margaret's work is featured at the *Vision* exhibition at the Georg Jensen store in New York City.

1961
Francis J. Sperisen publishes *The Art of Lapidary,* featuring examples of Margaret's work.

Margaret participates in the landmark *International Exhibition of Modern Jewelry, 1890–1961,* organized by the Worshipful Company of Goldsmiths and the Victoria and Albert Museum and curated by Graham Hughes, in Goldsmiths' Hall in London. Among the three pendants, four rings, and one pin, she exhibits a crystal pendant with inset diamonds that is purchased by Goldsmiths' Hall for their permanent collection.

1962
Margaret and Eugene move to 525–527 Montclair Avenue in Oakland, California, on May 3. Bess and John Bovingdon share joint tenancy in the split-level home. John, a former economist, is renowned for his modern dance. Eugene purchases the remainder of the Bovingdon's share in the joint tenancy in 1966.

1964
Margaret dies at her own hand in San Francisco on March 19.

FIGURE 17
Margaret De Patta and Eugene Bielawski at home in Napa, c. 1957
Margaret De Patta Archives, Bielawski Trust, Point Richmond, California

This timeline of Margaret De Patta's life was compiled by Jennifer Shaifer, Windgate Fellow at the Oakland Museum of California, from information in OMCA's and other archives and from city, state, and federal records.

Bibliography

ARCHIVAL SOURCES

Margaret De Patta Papers, 1944–2000. Archives of American Art, Smithsonian Institution, Washington, D.C.

Margaret De Patta Archive. Oakland Museum of California, Oakland, California.

Margaret De Patta Archives. Bielawski Trust, Point Richmond, California.

ARTICLES, BOOKS, EXHIBITION CATALOGUES

Adamson, Glenn. "Thinking Through Craft." *American Craft* 7, no. 6 (December–January 2008): 90–92.

Benson, E. M. "The Chicago Bauhaus and Moholy-Nagy." *Magazine of Art* 31 (1938): 82–83.

Betts, Paul. *The Authority of Everyday Objects: A Cultural History of West German Industrial Design.* Berkeley and Los Angeles: University of California Press, 2004.

Bowlt, John E., ed. *Russian Art of the Avant Garde: Theory and Criticism, 1902–1934.* New York: Viking Press, 1976.

Bray, Hazel, ed. *The Jewelry of Margaret De Patta: A Retrospective Exposition, February 3–March 28, 1976.* Oakland, Calif.: Oakland Museum of California, 1976.

Bredendieck, Hin. "The Legacy of the Bauhaus." *Art Journal* 22, no. 1 (autumn 1962): 15–21.

Brown, Conrad. "The Second Annual Conference of American Craftsmen." *Craft Horizons* 18, no. 5 (September–October 1958): 13.

Campbell, David R. "Designer-Craftsmen USA 1960." *Craft Horizons* 20, no. 4 (July–August 1960): 12–27.

Cardinale, Robert, and Hazel Bray. "Margaret De Patta: Structure Concepts and Design Sources." *Metalsmith* 3, no. 2 (spring 1983): 11–15.

Caton, Joseph H. *The Utopian Vision of Moholy-Nagy.* Ann Arbor, Michigan: UMI Research Press, 1984.

Childers, Frankie Teague. "Napa Woman Turns Hobby of Handsome Jewelry into Thriving Business in Stores Throughout U.S." *Napa Register,* 9 July 1954.

Civelli, Helen. "Wedding Ring Starts Girl on Career." *San Francisco News,* 2 January 1940.

"Contemporary Jewelry by Margaret De Patta." *Arts & Architecture* 66, no. 9 (September 1949): 34.

Crowley, David, and Jane Pavitt. *Cold War Modern: Design 1945–1970.* London: V&A Publications, 2008.

Decker, Bernice Stevens. "Couple Make Sculptured Jewelry." *Christian Science Monitor,* 24 November 1958.

Defenbacher, Dan. "Designer Craftsmen of the West, 1957." *Craft Horizons* 17, no. 4 (July–August 1957): 33–37.

Decorative Arts: Official Catalog, Department of Fine Arts Division of Decorative Arts, Golden Gate International Exposition, San Francisco, 1939. San Francisco: H. S. Crocker Company, Inc. and Schwabackery-Frey Company, 1939.

De Patta, Margaret. "De Patta." *Arts & Architecture* 64, no. 7 (July 1947): 30, 31, 54.

———. "From the Inside." *The Palette* 32, no. 2 (spring 1952): 14–19.

———. "De Patta." *Design Quarterly* 33 (1955): 5–7.

———. "Jewelry for an Ever-Increasing Minority." *Metalsmith* 9 (winter 1989): 8. Reprint of "De Patta," *Arts & Architecture,* 1947.

"De Patta Silver at Orrefors." *Art Digest* 15, no. 27 (1 December 1940): 27.

Dungan, Eloise. "A Tribute to Margaret: An Artist Who Made the Ordinary Beautiful." *San Francisco News College Bulletin,* 22 July 1964, 35.

Eidelberg, Martin, ed. *Design 1935–1965: What Modern Was.* New York: Harry N. Abrams and Musée des Arts Décoratifs de Montréal, 1991.

Elkins, Michael. "Artist for Our Time." *Arts & Architecture* 62, no. 8 (August 1945): 39, 40, 55–56.

Englebrecht, Lloyd C., and Peter Hahn. *50 Jahre New Bauhaus: Bauhausnachfolge in Chicago.* Berlin: Bauhaus-Archiv, Museum für Gestaltung, 1987.

"Farmhouse Turned into Modern Home." *Napa Register,* 26 January 1957.

Findeli, Alain. "Moholy-Nagy's Design Pedagogy in Chicago (1937–46)." *Design Issues* 7, no. 1 (autumn 1990): 4–19.

———. *Le Bauhaus de Chicago: L'oeuvre pédagogique de László Moholy-Nagy.* Sillery, Québec: Septentrion, 1995.

"First National Conference, ACC, Asilomar." *Craft Horizons* 17, no. 4 (July–August 1957): 17–32.

"Five Contemporary Jewelers." *Craft Horizons* 14, no. 4 (July–August 1954): 32–35.

Frosh, Judy. "Francis Sperisen: Master Lapidary." *American Craft* 45, no. 1 (February–March 1985): 40–43.

Galison, Peter. "Aufbau/Bauhaus: Logical Positivism and Architectural Modernism." *Critical Inquiry* 16, no. 4 (summer 1990): 709–52.

Glass, Laurie. "The Jewelry of Margaret De Patta." *Artweek* 7, no. 10 (6 March 1976): 9.

Gough, Maria. *The Artist as Producer: Russian Constructivism in Revolution.* Berkeley and Los Angeles: University of California Press, 2005.

Gray, Camilla. *The Russian Experiment in Art, 1863–1922.* London: Thames and Hudson, 1986.

Greenbaum, Toni. "The Studio Jewelry Movement: 1940–1980, Roots and Results." In *One of a Kind: American Studio Jewelry Today.* Edited by Susan Grant Lewin. New York: Harry N. Abrams, 1994.

———. *Messengers of Modernism: American Studio Jewelry 1940–1960.* Edited by Martin Eidelberg. Montreal: Montreal Museum of Decorative Arts in association with Flammarion, Paris and New York, 1996.

———. "Constructivism and American Studio Jewelry." *Studies in the Decorative Arts* 6, no. 1 (fall–winter 1998–1999): 68–94.

———. "Body Sculpture: California Jewelry." In *California Design: The Legacy of West Coast Craft and Style.* Edited by Suzanne Baizerman and Jo Lauria. San Francisco: Chronicle Books, 2005.

Greenbaum, Toni, and Pat Kirkham. "Women Jewelry Designers." In *Women Designers in the USA, 1900–2000: Diversity and Difference.* Edited by Pat Kirkham. New Haven: Yale University Press, 2000.

Gropius, Walter. *The New Architecture and the Bauhaus.* Cambridge: MIT Press, 1965.

Halverstadt, Hal. "American Jewelry 1963." *Craft Horizons* 23, no. 2 (March–April 1963): 23–34, 50–51.

Hodel, Emilia. "Local Art Colony: Margaret De Patta, Bergmann and Becker Find Expression in Metal Work." *San Francisco News*, 6 December 1946.

James-Chakraborty, Kathleen. *Bauhaus Culture: From Weimar to the Cold War.* Minneapolis: University of Minnesota Press, 2006.

"Jewelry, Past and Present." *Craft Horizons* 17, no. 6 (November–December 1957): 47.

"Jewels in Modern Setting: Margaret de Patta Creates a Challenge." *California Arts & Architecture* 57, no. 9 (September 1940): 18.

Karlstrom, Paul J., ed. *On the Edge of America: California Modernist Art 1900–1950.* Berkeley and Los Angeles: University of California Press, in association with the Archives of American Art, Smithsonian Institution, and the Fine Arts Museums of San Francisco, 1996.

Kentgens-Craig, Margret. *The Bauhaus and America: First Contacts, 1919–1936.* Cambridge: MIT Press, 2001.

Kiaer, Christina. *Imagine No Possessions: The Socialist Objects of Russian Constructivism.* Cambridge: MIT Press, 2008.

Krauss, Rosalind. *Passages in Modern Sculpture.* Cambridge: MIT Press, 1977.

Liebes, Dorothy Wright. "Contemporary Decorative Arts." In *Decorative Arts: Official Catalog, Department of Fine Arts Division of Decorative Arts, Golden Gate International Exposition, San Francisco, 1939,* 7–8. San Francisco: H.S. Crocker Company, Inc., and Schwabackery-Frey Company, 1939.

Lodder, Christina. *Russian Constructivism.* New Haven: Yale University Press, 1983.

Loke, Margaret. "Comprising with Light (No Camera Required)." *New York Times,* 26 February 1999.

Manhart, Marcia, Tom Manhart, and Carol Haralson. *The Eloquent Object: The Evolution of American Art in Craft Media since 1945.* Tulsa, Okla.: Philbrook Museum of Art, 1987.

Margolin, Victor. *The Struggle for Utopia: Rodchenko, Lissitzky, Moholy-Nagy, 1917–1946.* Chicago: University of Chicago Press, 1997.

Martin, John Leslie. "László Moholy-Nagy and the Chicago Institute of Design." *Architectural Review* 101 (1947): 224–26.

The Metal Experience: June 5–July 4, 1971. Oakland, Calif.: Oakland Museum, 1971.

Milner, John. *Vladimir Tatlin and the Russian Avant-Garde.* New Haven: Yale University Press, 1983.

"Modern Jewelry under Fifty Dollars." *Everyday Art Quarterly* 7 (spring 1948): 6–13.

Moholy-Nagy, László. *Vision in Motion.* Chicago: Paul Theobald, 1947.

Moholy-Nagy, László. "Constructivism and the Proletariat." In *Moholy-Nagy, An Anthology.* Edited by Richard Kostelanetz. Cambridge, Mass.: Da Capo Press, 1970.

Moholy-Nagy, Sibyl. *Moholy-Nagy: Experiment in Totality.* Cambridge: MIT Press, 1971.

Orr-Cahall, Christina, ed. *The Art of California: Selected Works from the Collection of the Oakland Museum.* San Francisco: Chronicle Books, 1984.

Prip, John, and Ronald Pearson. "Metals: Panel Discussion." *Craft Horizons* 26, no.3 (May–June 1966): 29, 31.

Pullman, Kay. "Oregon Ceramic Studio." *Craft Horizons* 20, no. 5 (September–October 1960): 36–37.

Resnikoff, Florence. "Northern California: A Center for Experimental Jewelry." *Craft Horizons* 16, no. 5 (September–October 1956): 26–29.

Ro, Jane. "Margaret De Patta: Floating Stones." *American Society of Jewelry Historians Newsletter* 24, no. 3 (winter 2010): 3–6.

Rockefeller, Barbara, ed. *Masterworks of Contemporary American Jewelry: Sources and Concepts.* London: Victoria and Albert Museum, 1985.

Rosenthal, Mildred. "Active Arts Demonstrator, Golden Gate International Exposition San Francisco 1940." *San Francisco Art Association Bulletin* 6, no. 9 (April 1940): 5.

Schiro, Anne-Marie. "Innovative Jewelry: 1940–1960." *New York Times,* 15 January 1985.

Schon, Marbeth. *Form and Function: American Modernist Jewelry, 1940–1970.* Atglen, Penn.: Schiffer Publishing, 2008.

Slowey, Anne. "Modern Times." *Elle* (USA) 22, no. 9 (May 2007): 194.

Sperisen, Francis J. *The Art of the Lapidary.* Milwaukee: Bruce Publishing Company, 1971.

Structure and Ornament: American Modernist Jewelry 1940–1960. New York: Fifty-50, 1984.

Turner, Ralph. *Jewelry in Europe and America: New Times, New Thinking.* London: Thames and Hudson, 1996.

"'Two Heads Better Than One' Couple Declares: Bielawskis, Faculty Husband-Wife Team in Art." *Summer Signal,* 8 July 1947.

Uchida, Yoshiko. "Letter from San Francisco." *Craft Horizons* 22, no. 2 (March–April 1962): 42.

———. "Margaret De Patta, 1903–1964." *Craft Horizons* 24, no. 4 (July–August 1964): 10.

———. "Jewelry by Margaret De Patta." *Craft Horizons* 25, no. 2 (March–April 1965): 22–25.

———. "Margaret De Patta." In *The Jewelry of Margaret De Patta: A Retrospective Exposition, February 3–March 28, 1976.* Edited by Hazel Bray. Oakland, Calif.: Oakland Museum of California, 1976.

"U.S. Crafts at Brussels." *Craft Horizons* 18, no. 3 (May–June 1958): 20–21.

Wick, Rainer K. *Teaching at the Bauhaus.* Ostfildern-Ruit, Germany: Hatje Cantz, 2000.

Wingler, Hans. *Bauhaus.* Cambridge: MIT Press, 1969.

Wise, Richard W. "Secrets of the Gem Trade: Margaret De Patta and the American Lapidary Renaissance." *Modern Silver* (2003), "http://www.modernsilver.com/secretsofthegemtrade.htm"

Wolf, Toni Lesser. Introduction to *Masterworks of Contemporary American Jewelry: Sources and Concepts.* London: Victoria and Albert Museum, 1985.

Zhadova, Larisa. *Tatlin.* London: Thames and Hudson, 1988.

Index

Page numbers for images are indicated in **boldface** type.

A

Akron Art Museum, 28

Albers, Anni, 57, 65, 134

Albers, Josef, 57

Amberg-Hirth, 110, 131

American Craft Council, 49

American Craftsmen's Council
Asilomar: The First Annual Conference of American Craftsmen, 46, 49, 138; *Dimensions of Design* conference, 138; *Designer-Craftsmen U.S.A. 1960* exhibition, 139

American Craftsmen's Educational Council, *Designer-Craftsmen U.S.A. 1953* traveling exhibition, 136

American Federation of Arts, *Creative Jewelry 1955–57* traveling exhibition, 136

American Jewelry and Other Objects exhibition, 136

Arnautoff, Victor, 134

Arp, Jean, 42

Art Copper Shop, 19, 131

Art Institute of Chicago, 26, 30

Art of Lapidary, The, 139

Art Students League, 18, 131

Arts & Architecture, 42, 109, 118, **120,** 121, 135

Asawa, Ruth, **137**

Asilomar: The First Annual Conference of American Craftsmen, 46, 49, 138

Association of Arts and Industries in Chicago, 26

B

Ball State Teachers College, 136

Bauhaus
in Germany, 17, 26, 31, 57
in the United States, 17, 26, 28, 31, 35, 44, 57, 132

Bauhaus-Archiv, 32

Bauhaus, How It Worked exhibition, 31, 132

Becker, Gerhard, 134

Bennett, Ward, 134

Bergmann, Franz, 132, 134, 136

Bertoia, Harry, 135

Bielawski, Eugene
California Labor School 34, 44, 45, 110, 134
Designs Contemporary, 42, 109, 110, 112, 118, 121, 122, 134, 138
Japan and Hong Kong, 50, **50,** 139
political agenda, 35, 45, 65, 110, 134
marriage to Margaret De Patta, 34, 134
Metal Arts Guild, 46, 136
Margaret De Patta Memorial Service, 51
Napa, 45, 134, 136, 138, **138, 139**
political agenda, 35, 45, 65, 110, 134
School of Design, 34, 110, 132

Biomorphism, 22, 63, 41, 42,

Black Mountain College, 57

Black, Starr & Gorham, **120,** 121

Blauvelt, Elizabeth Carolyn, 130

Boccioni, Umberto, 63

Bollman, Floyd Charlous, 130

Bolotowsky, Ilya, **30,** 31

Bovingdon, Bess and John, 139

Boyd Britton, 121

Brancusi, Constantin, 63

Brooklyn Museum, *Designer Craftsmen U.S.A. 1953* exhibition, 136

Brussels World's Fair *(Expo 58: Exposition Universelle et Internationale de Bruxelles),* 49, 138

Brynner, Irena, 46, 49, 131, 136, 138

Busch-Reisinger Museum, 65

C

Calder, Alexander, 42, 49, 63, 134

California College of Arts and Crafts, 137

California Design exhibitions, 124

California Labor School, 34, 44, **44,** 45, 46, 48, 51, 53 n45, 110, 132, 134, 135

California Pacific International Exposition in San Diego, 131

California Palace of the Legion of Honor, 18, 132, 136 (San Francisco Arts Festival)

California School of Fine Arts in San Francisco, 18, 130

California Senate Fact-Finding Committee on Un-American Activities (SUAC), 45, 110

California State Fair, 136

Cargoes, 112

Cartier, 49

Centro Escolar Revolución, 26, **27**

Constructivism, 22, 57, 58, 63, 65–66, 68, 71

Contemporary American Jewelry exhibition, 136

Contemporary Jewelry exhibition, 139

Creative Jewelry, 1955–1957 traveling exhibition, 136

Cross, Adelyne, 134

Cubism, Cubists, 19

Cunningham, Imogen, 137

D

Davis, Adelle, 137

de Diego, Julio, 134

De Patta, Margaret, **16, 27, 50, 130–31, 133–35, 137–39**
education, 18, 19, 26, 31, **32,** 33, 35–36, 38, 58, 60, 130, 131, 132
Metal Arts Guild, 46, 136
political agenda, 71, 110, 134
residences, 34, **34,** 45–46, **45, 50,** 131, 132, 136, 138, 139
teaching, 44–45, 132, 134, 137
travel 26, **27,** 31, 50, 131, 139

De Patta, Salvatore (Sam), 19, 26, **27,** 31, 34, 131, 132

De Stijl, 63

Designer Craftsmen U.S.A. 1953 traveling exhibition, 136

Designer Craftsmen U.S.A. 1960 exhibition, 139

Designs Contemporary, 42, 47, **108,** 109, **109,** 110, 112, 118, **119,** 121, 122, 124, 126 n4, 134

Detroit Institute of Arts, *An Exhibition for Modern Living,* 135

Dimensions of Design conference, 138

Dixon, Harry, 46, 136

E

Eames, Charles, 122, 124

Eames, Ray, 122

Ehrman, Marli, 31, 132

Evans, Edward S., Jr., 123

Everyday Art Quarterly, 118

Exhibition for Modern Living, 135

F

Falkenstein, Claire, 134, 135

Fine Arts Gallery in San Diego, 136

Futurists, 19, 63

G

Gabo, Naum, 63, **64**

Georg Jensen, *Vision* exhibition, 47, 139

George Eastman House, International Museum of Photography and Film, 41, 58, 67

Gilbert, Louise, 134

Golden Gate International Exposition, 1939, 22, 131, 132

Goldsmiths' Hall, *International Exhibition of Modern Jewellery, 1890–1961,* 49, 139

Good Design exhibitions, 124

H

Hairenian, Armin, 19, 131

Halberstadt, Milton, **8,** 41, **41, 134**

Heath, Edith Kiertzner, 48, 65, 134, 136, 139

Heath Ceramics, 139

Hesse, Eva, 60

Hickok Manufacturing Company, 118, 136

Hughes, Graham, 139

Huntington Galleries, *American Jewelry and Related Objects* exhibition, 136

I

Illinois Institute of Technology, 58, 132

Institute of Design, 58, 132

International Design Competition for Sterling Silver Flatware, 47, **47,** 139

International Exhibition of Modern Jewellery, 1890–1961, 49, 139

Iowa State Teachers College, *Annual Invitational Show,* 136

J

Jewelry by Margaret De Patta Bielawski exhibition, 137

K

Kaplan, Louis, 63

Kepes, György, 31, 132

Kineticism, 31, 60, 41, **41,** 58, 60, **62,** 66, 71, **70**

Koblick, Freda, 134

Kramer, Sam, 135

L

Lalique, 49

Life magazine, 124

Lipschitz, Jacques, 134

Lissitzky, El, 57, 63, 68, **68**

Lobel, Paul, 134, 135

Long Beach Museum of Art, *Jewelry, Past and Present* exhibition, 49, 138

Los Angeles County Fair Association, *The Arts in Western Living* traveling exhibition, 136, 137

Loska, Mary Margaret, 130

M

Macchiarini, Peter, 46, 126 n2, 134, 136

Macchiarini, Virginia, 136

Malevich, Kazimir, 57

Man Ray, 60

Margaret De Patta Memorial Exhibition, 50–51

Mermod, Jaccard & King Jewelry Company, 121

Metal Arts Guild, 46, 51, 90, 136; *Jewelry, Past and Present* exhibition, 138

Miller, John Paul, 49, 138

Miller, Kenneth Hayes, 18, 131

Mills College, 31, 132; Art Department, 136; Art Gallery, 18, 31, 52-fn3

Milwaukee-Downer College, *Contemporary Jewelry* exhibition, 139

Modern Handmade Jewelry, 42, 110, 134

Modern Jewelry Under Fifty Dollars exhibition, 43, 135

Moholy-Nagy, László, 17, 26, 28, 31, 33, **33,** 38, **40,** 41, 44, 57, 58, **58,** 60, **60,** 63, 65, 66, **67,** 131, 132

Mondrian, Piet, 52 n35, 63,

Montgomery Ward, 122

Montreal Museum of Fine Arts, 37, 38, 83, 86, 88, 96, 116

Morris, Robert, 60

Museum of Arts and Design, 49, 137, 139

Museum of Contemporary Crafts
 Craftsmanship in a Changing World exhibition, 49, 137
 Designer Craftsmen U.S.A. 1960 exhibition, 139

Museum of Modern Art, 61, 69
 The Bauhaus: How It Worked exhibition, 31, 132
 Good Design exhibitions, 124
 Modern Handmade Jewelry traveling exhibition, 42, 110, 134

Myers, Barbara Cannon, **16**

N

Nanny's, 112, 121

New Bauhaus, *see* Bauhaus.

New Yorker, **120,** 121

Niedringhaus, Charles, 31, 132

O

Oakland Art Gallery, *European Modernists* exhibition, 18, 52 n3

Oakland Museum of California, 52-fn3

Oberlin College, Dudley Peter Allen Memorial Art Museum, *Contemporary American Jewelry* exhibition, 136

Ohio State University in Columbus, *Jewelry by Margaret De Patta Bielawski* exhibition, 137

Opticuts, 36, 58, 122

Oregon Ceramic Studio, 135

P

Pacific Arts Association, 1939 conference, 26

Pacific Shop, **120**

Palace of Fine Arts, 131

Palette, The, 136

Panama-Pacific International Exposition, 18

Pasadena Art Museum, *California Design* exhibitions, 124

Patri, Giacomo, 51, 134

Pebble and stone jewelry, 40, 41, **69, 96, 97**

Pineda, Antonio, 132

Pevsner, Anton, 57

Photograms, 28, **28, 29, 43,** 60, **61,** 63

Picasso, Pablo, 42, 49

Popova, Lyubov, 57

Portland Art Museum, 134

Pousette-Dart, Richard, 134

Prestini, James, 31

Primitivism, 19

R

Radakovich, Ruth and Svetozar, 49

Rebajes, Francisco, **30,** 31

Renk, Merry, 46, 131, 136

Resnikoff, Florence, 131

Richmond Art Center, exhibition, 136

Rodchenko, Alexander, 57, 60, **62,** 63, 65

Rolette, Romeo, **133**

Rosene, Caroline, 46, 136

S

San Diego High School, 130

San Diego Academy of Fine Arts, 18, 130

Sandoz, Gérard, 66

San Francisco Arts Festival, 136

San Francisco Art Commission, San Francisco Arts Festival, 136

San Francisco Museum of Art, *Margaret De Patta Memorial Exhibition,* 51

Scheyer, Galka, 52, fn 3

Schmidt, Christian, 49

School of Design (Chicago), 26, 31, **32, 33,** 33, 34, 58, 132

Schuster, William, 130

Sears, Roebuck and Company, 122

Shattuck School, 134

Slutzky, Naum, 65, **66**

Smith, Art, 135

Smithsonian American Art Museum, 84

Sperisen, Francis, 35, **35,** 36, 131, 136, 139

Stepanova, Varvara, 57

Strong, Adelia Frances, 130

Strong, Charlotte Pauline, 130

Strong, Harold Meade, 130

Strong, Mary Margaret, 18, 130

T

Tacoma Art Museum, 117

Tatlin, Vladimir, 57, 65

Thirty-four American Artists, 136

Tiffany, 49

Tom Mooney Labor School, *see* California Labor School.

U

University of California, 45

University of Minnesota, University Gallery, *34 American Artists* exhibition, 136

University of Oregon, 134

V

Van Doesburg, Theo, 63

Van Keppel-Green, 112, 12

Vision exhibition, 139

Victoria and Albert Museum, *International Exhibition of Modern Jewellery, 1890–1961,* 49, 66

Vision and Individual Response seminar, 138

VKhUTEMAS, 57

Von Neumann, Robert, 49

von Schlegell, William, 131

W

Walker Art Center
 Everyday Art Quarterly, 118
 Everyday Gallery, 42, 84
 Contemporary Jewelers exhibition, 136
 Modern Jewelry Under Fifty Dollars exhibition, 43, 135

Walter Wright, 121

Western Association of Art Museum Directors, 138

Winston, Bob, 46, 135, 136

Wolff, Robert Jay, 31

Wong, Jade Snow, 136

World's Fair, Brussels, 49, 138; New York, 31, 131

Worshipful Company of Goldsmiths, *International Exhibition of Modern Jewellery, 1890–1961,* 49, 139

Photo Credits

Photo courtesy of Akron Museum of Art, 28

Photo courtesy of Andrea Rosen Gallery: 60 (both)

Photography © The Art Institute of Chicago, 30 (top)

© 2011 Artist Rights Society (ARS), New York VG Bild-Kunst, Berlin: 40, 58, 60 (both), 67 (bottom), 68

Photo courtesy of Bauhaus-Archiv Berlin: 33 (top)

© Black, Starr & Frost: 120 (upper right)

Photo by Benjamin Blackwell: 8, 16, 18, 27 (both), 32, 33 (bottom), 35 (top), 44, 47 (both), 48 (top and bottom left), 79, 83 (left), 108, 109, 111 (top), 112, 119, 120 (bottom), 123, 130, 131 (both), 132 (left), 133 (right), 134 (left), 135 (both), 137, endpapers

© 2011 The Imogen Cunningham Trust. www.ImogenCunningham.com, 137

Photo courtesy of Dallas Museum of Art, 105

Photo by M. Lee Fatherree: 2, 10, 20 (left), 21, 22, 25, 36, 43 (upper left, upper right and lower left), 59, 64 (bottom), 67 (top), 70, 77, 78, 80, 81, 82 (both), 84 (bottom), 85, 93, 97, 98, 99 (all), 100, 102 (both), 103, 114 (lower right), 116 (top and lower left), 125 (lower), 132 (right), back cover (lower right)

Photo courtesy of George Eastman House, International Museum of Photography and Film: 40, 58, 67 (bottom)

Photo courtesy of Goldsmiths' Hall, London: 49

Photo by Christine Guest, MMFA: 37, 38, 83 (right), 86, 88, 96, 114 (upper right), 115 (upper right), 116 (bottom right)

© The M. Halberstadt Family Trust. All rights reserved. 8, 41, 134 (lower right), back cover (top)

© President and Fellows of Harvard College, photo by Junius Beebe: 64

Photo by Eva Heyd: 69

Photo by Robin Hill: 39, 43 (middle), 87

Photo courtesy of Patricia Riveron Lee: 30 (bottom)

Photo by Hattula Moholy-Nagy: 91

© 2011 Museum Associates/LACMA: 89 (bottom)

© 2012 Museum of Fine Arts, Boston: 89 (top), 117 (bottom)

© Barbara Cannon Myers. All rights reserved: front cover, 16

Photo by Romeo Rolette: 34 (upper and lower right), 131 (left), 133 (right)

Photo by Siegelson, New York: 20 (bottom)

Photo by Eric Smith, courtesy of Metal Arts Guild, San Francisco: 90

Photo courtesy of Smithsonian American Art Museum, photo by Gene Young: 84

Photo courtesy of Smithsonian Archives of American Art: 50

Photo courtesy of Tacoma Art Museum, photo by Richard Nicol: 117 (top left and top right)

Photo by John Bigelow Taylor: 23, 24, 24, 29, 62 (right), 92, 95, 101, 104, 125 (top), back cover (lower left)

© David Travers: 120 (lower left)

Photo courtesy of Ubu Gallery, New York & Barry Friedman Limited, New York: 29 (top), 61 (both)

© Victoria and Albert Museum, London: 66

© Nina & Graham Williams: 64 (upper right)

Captions

FRONTISPIECE
Margaret De Patta
Pin, 1954
white gold, sterling silver, smoky quartz, pearl
2½ x 1⅞ x ½ in. (63.5 x 47.6 x 12.7 mm)
Collection of Ruth Asawa

PAGE 6
Margaret De Patta
Jewelry as photographed by the artist, c. 1941
Margaret De Patta Archives, Bielawski Trust, Point Richmond, California

PAGE 8
Milton Halberstadt (1919—2000)
Margaret De Patta production jewelry, 1947
Margaret De Patta Archives, Bielawski Trust, Point Richmond, California

PAGE 10
Margaret De Patta
"Margaret" wedding band, 1946
sterling silver
⅜ x ⅞ in. (10 x 22 mm)
Collection of the Oakland Museum of California, Gift of Eugene Bielawski, The Margaret De Patta Memorial Collection

PAGES 14-15
Margaret De Patta
Drawing of wire structure and crystals, c. 1955–60
graphite on paper
4¾ x 7 in. (12.1 x 17.8 cm)
Margaret De Patta Archives, Bielawski Trust, Point Richmond, California

PAGES 54-55
Margaret De Patta
Drawing for pin, c. 1945
graphite on paper
3½ x 6 in. (8.9 x 15.2cm)
Margaret De PattaArchives, Bielawski Trust, Point Richmond, California

PAGES 74-75
Margaret De Patta
Working drawing for Mrs. Johnson, c. 1950
graphite on paper
5½ x 6¾ in. (13.9 x 17.2 cm)
Margaret De Patta Archives, Bielawski Trust, Point Richmond, California

PAGES 106-7
Margaret De Patta
Drawing for rutilated crystal ring, c. 1946
graphite on paper
3 x 5 in. (7.6 x 12 cm)
Margaret De Patta Archives, Bielawski Trust, Point Richmond, California

PAGES 128-29
Margaret De Patta
Working sketch, c. 1940–50
graphite on paper
6¼ x 9½ in. (15.9 x 24.1 cm)
Margaret De Patta Archives, Bielawski Trust, Point Richmond, California

All measurements: height x width x depth, unless otherwise noted.